Served In Salem

A Cookbook
presented by
The Ladies Committee
of the
Essex Institute
Salem, Massachusetts 01970

Library of Congress Catalog Card Number 82-71659

ISBN 0-88389-083-6

Photographs: Mark Sexton

Illustrations: Lynn St. Clair

Printed by

Deschamps Printing Co., Inc.

Salem, Massachusetts 01970

COVER PICTURE — AFTERNOON TEA

Tea time in colonial Salem was an important event. A Chinese export porcelain tea set is complemented by handsomely carved Massachusetts Chippendale furniture and portraits of sea captains.

FARE

THE COOKBOOK COMMITTEE

Edna Lail, Co-chairman
Rilda Stuart, Co-chairman

Hazel Breed
Caroline Cahoon
Peggy-Jo Chagan
Lucy Conley
Andrea Cox
Dorothy Creamer
Maureen Donovan
Helen Goodhue
Virginia Hazen
Grace Morrison
Mary Moulton

Joan Osgood
Marion Peirson
Reinette Phillips
Beth Pratt
Nancy Pocharski
Barbara Roper
Lynn St. Clair
Carol Smith
Polly Townsend
Ruth West
Jeri Zelinski

FOREWORD

The Essex Institute, established in 1848, is one of this country's oldest, largest, and most widely recognized privately endowed regional historical societies. The Institute owns and maintains fourteen buildings which are listed on the National Register of Historic Places; three of our houses are National Historic Landmarks. Contained in these buildings are a major research library of printed and manuscript materials, a museum collection of nearly 40,000 objects, historic period rooms covering the period 1680 to 1870, and Institute offices for education, public relations, maintenance and conservation, and publications.

During the year, the Institute offers lectures, exhibition openings, scholarly meetings, musical performances, films, special tours, education classes, social functions, and other events. These programs and activities are focused on the Institute's prime raison d'etre — to chronicle and document the life and culture of Essex County, Massachusetts, one of the most historically rich regions in the northeastern United States.

Since its formation in 1968, the Essex Institute Ladies Committee has been an important part of the Institute. The Committee's stated purpose is to promote the welfare and membership of the Institute, and to encourage public participation in its affairs. One of the Committee's primary functions is to provide financial support to the Institute through special fund-raising projects and events. The Committee's principal project for 1981-82 has been the compilation and production of this book of Salem recipes. The Institute is greatly indebted to the Committee and to the many contributors who helped to make the book possible. Our museum and library have interesting collections of culinary artifacts and old recipes, and hence it is highly appropriate that an illustrated cookbook, the first of its kind for Salem, appear under the auspices of the Essex Institute. I am confident that this publication will be a valuable addition to your own kitchen library and perhaps that of a friend. We hope you will enjoy reading the book and sampling these recipes, old and new, which have been contributed and tested by some of the finest cooks in the Salem area!

Bryant F. Tolles, Jr.
Director and Librarian
Essex Institute

INTRODUCTION

A delightful, beautifully conceived benefit, presented in the spring of 1981, led directly to the compiling and publishing of this cookbook, *Served in Salem*. The Ladies Committee of the Essex Institute, Salem, Massachusetts, with awareness of the rich historical and cultural heritage of the Salem area, yearly sponsor events which reflect the uniqueness of this New England region. Striking photographs of an outstanding exhibit of period table settings taken at the benefit, "The Joy of Dining as Shown in Art," inspired the undertaking of this book.

The Ladies Committee is pleased to share this cookbook of treasured recipes that have been collected over the years, many of which have been passed down through generations of fine cooks in the homes along the shore north of Boston.

Proceeds from this book will be presented to the Essex Institute and used to insure the continued support of this multifaceted historical society.

All those who so kindly contributed to *Served in Salem* are gratefully acknowledged by the Committee.

hors d'oeuvres

Copied from a weathervane by Thomas Drowne - 1771 - ordered by Richard Derby for the East Church, Salem. The vane is often referred to by Dr. William Bentley, who was pastor of the church 1785-1819, in his famous diary.

Collection of the Essex Institute, Salem

ARTICHOKE DIP

1 8-oz. can artichoke hearts,
   drained and chopped
Garlic powder to taste

1 cup mayonnaise
1 cup Paramesan cheese

Blend ingredients in ovenproof serving dish. Bake at 350° for 20 minutes.
Serve hot with crackers.

HOT BROCCOLI DIP

2 pkgs. frozen chopped broccoli,
   cooked and drained
1 cup finely chopped onion
1 cup finely chopped celery
1 tbls. butter or margarine

1 4-oz. can mushroom pieces
1 roll garlic cheese
1 can cream of mushroom soup
Tabasco sauce

Sauté onions and celery in butter until soft (not brown). Add mushrooms,
cheese, and soup. Heat until well blended. Add broccoli; add Tabasco sauce
to taste. Heat until bubbly. Serve hot in chafing dish with corn chips. May
be made ahead and reheated.

HOT CRAB DIP

8 oz. cream cheese
1 can king crabmeat
1 tbls. Worcestershire
Dash Tabasco

1 tsp. dry onion flakes
1 tbls. lemon juice
2 tsps. blue cheese
2 oz. sherry

Put all ingredients into mixing bowl; beat with electric mixer just until well
blended. Pile into small casserole or cheese crock and bake at 350° for one-
half hour. Serve with potato chips or crackers. May be made a day ahead.
Serves 8 to 10.

GUACAMOLE

1 onion, small, chopped	¼ tsp. white pepper
2 medium-ripe avocadoes, chopped	1 tsp. salt
1 medium tomato, peeled, seeds	¼ tsp. sugar
removed, chopped	2 tbls. mayonnaise
1½ tsps. lemon juice	

In food processor, chop onion with steel blade; add avocadoes, and chop for 5-10 seconds; add tomato, and chop for 5 seconds. Add seasonings; turn on and off immediately. Put in small bowl, cover with the mayonnaise, and refrigerate, at least one half hour. Before serving, mix in the mayonnaise. Serve with corn or tortilla chips. Do not freeze.

CURRY SHRIMP DIP

2 8-oz. pkgs. cream cheese,	1 tbls. curry powder
softened	1 small onion, grated
1 can cream of shrimp soup	1 6-oz. pkg. small shrimp

Blend all ingredients. Bake at 350° for 20 minutes. Serve hot with crackers.

SPRING FANTASY DIP

1 8-oz. pkg. cream cheese	1 beaten egg
1 3-oz. pkg. cream cheese	1 tbls. vinegar
¼ cup minced green pepper	1 tbls. sugar
¼ cup minced onion	

Soften cream cheese. Mix egg, vinegar, and sugar together, and add to cheese. Beat until well mixed and creamy. Add green pepper and onion. Chill. May be frozen. Serve with corn chips as dippers.

SUMMER DAYS' DIP

1 12-oz. carton (1½ cups) cream-style cottage cheese	1½ tsp. paprika
	¾ tsp. garlic salt
2 tbls. mayonnaise or salad dressing	Dash of pepper
	1 tbls. lemon juice

Put all ingredients into blender, and blend until smooth. Chill. Top with parsley. Serve with carrot sticks, other raw vegetables, or chips.

CHEESE BALL

10-oz. pkg. soft cheddar	1 tbls. mustard
8-oz. pkg. cream cheese	1 tbls. onion salt
2-, 3-, or 4-oz. pkg. blue cheese	¼ tsp. garlic salt

Soften cheeses and mix with mustard and salts. (If mixture seems too stiff, add a few drops of Sherry.) Form into a ball, and refrigerate several hours.

Coating: 1 3-oz. pkg. cream cheese
2 tbls. horseradish
Chopped parsley leaves

Mix cheese and horseradish. Cover all except the bottom of the cheese ball. Place on saucer; cover with saran; refrigerate overnight. To serve, cover with chopped parsley and surround with Melba rounds or crackers.

JANE'S CHEESE BALL

1 4-oz. pkg. blue cheese	2 tbls. A1 sauce
1 5-oz. jar processed cheddar cheese	1 cup pecans, finely chopped
1 8-oz. pkg. cream cheese	2 tbls. parsley flakes
1 small onion, grated	

Mix with electric mixer the three cheeses, grated onion, and the A1 sauce. Chill until mixture can be formed into a ball. Roll ball in pecans and parsley. May be divided into 3 small balls. May be frozen.

SHRIMP CHEESE BALLS

2 3-oz. pkgs. cream cheese, softened
1 4½-oz. can (¾ cup) shrimp
½ tsp. prepared mustard
1 tsp. grated onion

1 tsp. lemon juice
Dash cayenne pepper
Dash of salt
⅔ cup chopped, salted nuts

Blend mustard, onion, lemon juice, pepper, and salt into cheese. Drain shrimp well; break into pieces; stir into cheese mix. Chill. Form into ½-inch balls. Roll in chopped, salted nuts. Makes 3½ dozen balls.

OLIVE AND CHEESE BALL

1 8-oz. pkg. cream cheese
8 oz. Blue cheese, crumbled
¼ cup soft butter or margarine
⅔ cup (4½-oz. can) well drained,
  chopped ripe olives

1 tsp. minched chives
⅓ cup chopped walnuts or toasted,
  diced almonds

Soften cheeses, and blend with butter. Stir in olives and chives. Chill slightly for easier shaping. Form into ball. Chill thoroughly. Just before serving, sprinkle ball with chopped nuts. Trim with parsley. Serve with assorted crackers. Makes 3 cups. May be frozen.

FANCY CHICKEN LOG

2 8-oz. pkgs. cream cheese, softened
1 tbls. bottled steak sauce
½ tsp. curry powder
1½ cups cooked chicken, minced

⅓ cup minced celery
¼ cup chopped parsley
¼ cup blanched almonds, chopped
small jar of pimientoes

Mix together cheese, steak sauce, and curry powder. Blend in chicken, celery, and 2 tablespoons of the parsley. Shape into a 9-inch log. Wrap in plastic wrap, and chill 4 hours or overnight. Toss together remaining parsley and almonds. Cover log with this mixture. Thinly slice some pimiento strips and place in diagonal fashion over log. Serve with crackers. Makes about 3 cups.

SILVER'S SPECIAL

1 3-oz. pkg. cream cheese	3-4 drops Tabasco
1 egg yolk	¼ tsp. dried tarragon (optional)
¼ - ½ tsp. curry powder	Unsalted crackers
Dash Worcestershire	

Soften cream cheese; mix with egg yolk thoroughly. Add curry powder, Worcestershire, and Tabasco. Add tarragon if desired. Spread mixture with moderate generosity on crackers; put on cookie sheet in 400° oven for about 10 minutes. Check to see that mixture puffs and becomes lightly browned. Do not allow to burn. Serve immediately. (Minced onions and/or other herbs may be used to vary flavor.)

OLD-FASHIONED CHEESE CRACKERS

Saltines	Grated Italian-style cheese
Butter	(Romano, Parmesan)

Arrange crackers on cookie sheet. Butter generously. Sprinkle about one teaspoon cheese over each cracker. Put in 350° oven for about 15 minutes, watching carefully to be sure they brown but do not burn.

ROKA CHEESE SPREAD

4 3-oz. pkgs. cream cheese	4 hard-boiled eggs, chopped
1 small bottle stuffed green olives with juice, chopped	1 jar Roka Cheese Spread
	½ tsp. grated onion

Blend cream and Roka cheeses together thoroughly; add chopped olives and juice; mix chopped eggs and onions; add to cheese mixture and blend well. Store in covered container in refrigerator. Serve with crackers. Better when made a day ahead.

GALA PECAN SPREAD

1 8-oz. pkg. cream cheese, softened
2 tbls. milk
1 2½-oz. jar dried beef, finely cut
¼ cup green pepper, finely chopped
2 tsps. onion flakes
½ tsp. garlic salt

¼ tsp. pepper
½ cup sour cream
2 tbls. butter/margarine
½ tsp. salt
½ cup pecans, coarsely chopped

Combine cheese and milk; mix well. Stir in chopped beef, green pepper, and dry seasonings. Add sour cream. Spoon into one large or two 6-inch oven-proof bowls. Combine chopped pecans, butter, and salt in skillet. Heat, stirring, until browned. Sprinkle nuts over mixture in bowl(s). Bake in 250° oven for 20 minutes. Serve hot with crackers. May be refrigerated overnight; if so, bake for 30 minutes.

HAM AND CHEESE SPREAD

1 2½-oz. can Deviled Ham
1 jar Olive & Pimiento Cheese
  Spread

Dash Worcestershire
1 tbls. minced onion
1 tsp. prepared mustard

Mix all ingredients well. Refrigerate at least two hours or overnight, covered. Serve with unsalted crackers.

HOMESTYLE BOURSIN

2 8-oz. pkgs. cream cheese, softened
¼ cup salad dressing
2 tsps. Dijon mustard

2 tbls. chopped chives, fresh or frozen
2 tbls. chopped dried dill
1 clove garlic, finely chopped

Using electric mixer, beat all ingredients until blended. Line two-cup mold or bowl with foil. Spoon mixture in; cover; refrigerate at least overnight. To serve: peel off foil, place on plate, surround with crackers. Will keep a week in refrigerator.

PIER 4 CHEESE SPREAD

¼ cup butter
¼ cup cream cheese
2 lbs. soft Cheddar cheese

1 tbls. Worcestershire Sauce
1 tbls. horseradish
2 tbls. sherry wine (dry or regular)

In mixer, blend cream cheese and butter. While mixing, add Cheddar cheese in small amounts until well blended. Add remaining ingredients until smooth and creamy. Refrigerate. Remove 1 hour before serving.

CHEESE PUFFS

6 slices firm white bread
¼ cup grated cheddar
2 tbls. grated onion

2 tbls. mayonnaise
2 tbls. bacon bits (optional)

Remove crusts from bread; toast; cut each slice into 4 squares or circles. Mix cheese, onion, and mayonnaise; add bacon bits if desired. Spread on toast. Place on cookie sheet, and bake in 350° oven until puffed and slightly browned.

SARA'S CHOPPED LIVER SPREAD

½ cup chicken fat or margarine
2 medium onions, sliced
½ lb. beef liver
½ lb. chicken livers

2 hard-boiled eggs
2-3 soda crackers
1 tsp. salt
Pepper to taste

Melt ¼ cup fat; sauté onions until golden; set aside. Melt rest of fat; sauté livers 5 to 10 minutes. Grind all ingredients or chop in chopping bowl; **do not use blender**. Grind crackers and eggs; add to liver and onion mix, reserving a tablespoon of egg to sprinkle over top. Mound on plate; sprinkle with egg; serve with crackers.

CAVIAR-EGG RING

6 hard-cooked eggs, riced
1 cup real mayonnaise
1 tsp. Worcestershire
Dash onion salt or powder

1 2-oz. jar Danish Caviar, black or red
2 tbls. lemon juice
2 tbls. water
1 tbls. plain gelatin

Mix lemon juice, water, and gelatin; stir over low heat until gelatin is dissolved. Mix remaining ingredients **except** caviar. Fold in caviar slowly. Pour into lightly oiled 6-cup ring mold. Let set in refrigerator 6 hours or overnight. Unmold and serve on unsalted crackers.

CRAB MOUSSE

2 7-oz. cans crabmeat
1 8-oz. pkg. cream cheese
1 10½-oz. can Cream of
   Mushroom Soup
¾ cup mayonnaise

1 small onion, finely minced
½ cup celery, finely chopped
2 tsp. minced chives
2 envelopes plain gelatin
¼ cup hot water

Dissolve gelatin in hot water. Heat soup, cream cheese, and mayonnaise together in saucepan; when blended, stir in dissolved gelatin; let cool. Add celery, onion, and chives. Add crabmeat which has been picked over carefully. Spoon into a lightly oiled 3½-cup mold. Chill in refrigerator 8 hours or overnight.

SHRIMP MOLD

1 can Cream of Tomato Soup
2 cans shrimp (or ½ lb. cooked
   small shrimp)
1 3-oz. pkg. cream cheese
¾ cup minced onion

¾ cup chopped celery
1 cup mayonnaise
1 tbls. plain gelatin
¼ cup water
1 tbls. Worcestershire

Heat soup; add gelatin which has been softened in water. Remove from heat. Add remaining ingredients. Pour into a 6-cup ring mold which has been rinsed in cold water. Chill until firm, at least 3 hours or overnight. Serve with crackers.

LIVER PATÉ MOLD

1 can beef bouillon
1 envelope plain gelatin
¼ cup cold water
2 tbls. sherry

1 can liver paté
1 8-oz. pkg. cream cheese
2 tbls. bourbon or brandy

Soak gelatin in cold water; add sherry and bouillon. Put half of this mixture in small bowl or mold and refrigerate until set. Mix liver paté, cream cheese, and bourbon or brandy until well blended. Spread over mixture in bowl. Cover with remaining bouillon mixture. Let set for several hours or overnight. Unmold. Serve with crackers.

BLUE CHEESE MEATBALLS

4 oz. blue cheese
¼ cup mayonnaise
2 tbls. Worcestershire
1 tsp. prepared mustard
salt and pepper to taste

2 cups cornflakes
½ cup milk
1 beaten egg
1 lb. ground meat

Mix all together; form into 60 small balls. Place on cookie sheet or large pan with sides (they are juicy). Bake at 350° for 20-25 minutes. Serve hot with toothpicks. May be frozen.

GLAZED BACON

1 lb. thick sliced bacon
¾ cup light brown sugar

2 tsps. ground cinnamon

Cut bacon package into 4 parts vertically. Separate pieces carefully. Mix cinnamon and sugar together on plate. Press pieces of bacon into mixture, coating both sides; shake off excess. Place on oven rack in foil-lined pans. Bake at 200° for one hour. Cool on racks for a few minutes. Place on paper towels; cover with additional paper towels to absorb grease. Pieces may be cut in half. Put bacon pieces in plastic box or foil container; put wax paper between layers of bacon. Cover container(s) with plastic wrap. Refrigerate or freeze until needed. To serve, put bacon pieces on pan in 200° oven and heat until warm. Drain on paper towels if necessary.

DINNER PARTY

In anticipation of a perfect evening the hostess surveys her elegantly appointed table. All is in readiness with the colorful flowers, cherished Baccarat crystal c. 1890 and gold crested Briggs & Co. china c. 1870.

Dinner Party

Crab Soup

Fillet of Beef

Spinach Ring with Mushrooms

Carrot Casserole

Dinner Rolls

Angel Pie

Strawberry Sauce

RED CAVIAR DIP

1 3-oz. pkg. cream cheese
½ cup sour cream

2 tbls. grated onion
½ cup red caviar

Soften cheese; beat with sour cream until light and fluffy. Blend in onion and caviar. Serve with chips, crackers or toast strips.

CALAMARI

1½ lbs. Squid
2 or 3 lemons, squeezed
½ tsp. garlic salt

½ tsp. oregano
2 tbls. olive oil
3 tbls. parsley, Italian preferred

Clean squid*, cut in one-inch squares, but leave tentacles whole. Cook in **just** enough water to cover for 20 minutes. Drain, but reserve dregs. Marinate squid and dregs in all other ingredients in refrigerator for the day. Serve in a bowl beside a plate of bread squares (1½" x 1½" approximately) and a small serving fork. Do not freeze.
*Edible parts of squid: 1) whole body with insides removed completely; 2) tentacles, cut off just in front of eyes; remove "tooth" from center of tentacles.

SARDINE SPREAD

2 3-oz. pkgs. cream cheese
3 tbls. heavy cream
2 tsps. prepared mustard
3 tbls. grated onion

¼ tsp. black pepper
1 7½-oz. can skinless, boneless
    sardines, drained and mashed

With electric mixer, beat cheese, cream, mustard and onions until very smooth. With paper towels, pat sardines as dry as possible before mashing. Blend sardines and pepper into other ingredients. Heap in serving bowl and refrigerate until ready to serve. Serve with corn chips or toast strips.

STUFFED BRUSSEL SPROUTS

1½ to 2 lbs. brussel sprouts
1 cup Italian salad dressing
½ cup cottage cheese

½ tsp. grated onion
2 oz. blue cheese, crumbled
½ tsp. seasoned salt

Cook brussel sprouts until crisp tender. With a sharp knife, remove center core from each sprout. Place shells upside down on paper towels to drain thoroughly (about 15 minutes). Place drained sprouts in bowl and pour salad dressing evenly over them. Cover and refrigerate 6 hours or overnight. Combine remaining ingredients. Spoon mixture evenly into sprout shells. Makes approximately 40.

STUFFED MUSHROOMS I

1½ tbls. finely diced onions
2 tbls. butter
¼ cup soft bread crumbs
¼ cup chopped walnuts
1½ tsp. chili sauce

1½ tsp. lemon juice
½ tsp. salt
Dash of pepper
6-8 large canned mushrooms

Cook onions in 1 tbls. of butter over low heat until tender but not brown. Stir in remaining ingredients except mushrooms. Stuff mushroom caps with mixture. Melt remaining tablespoon of butter and use to brush the mushroom caps. Broil until golden brown. Serve hot.

STUFFED MUSHROOMS II

¼ cup milk
3 drops onion juice
1 egg yolk
6-8 mushroom caps

2 tbls. cracker or bread crumbs
salt and pepper to taste
Mushroom stems, chopped

Heat milk to boiling point and pour over crumbs; add remaining ingredients. Stuff mushroom caps. Bake on flat pan at 350° for 8 to 10 minutes.

MARINATED MUSHROOMS

3 lbs. mushrooms washed and sliced.

Mix:

Pinch oregano	1 chopped onion
Pinch hot pepper	4 tsps. sugar
7 tsps. salt	1 pint wine vinegar
4 tsps. Accent	1 cup oil
¼ tsp. pepper	1 whole garlic, chopped
(white or black)	(more or less)

Boil all ingredients except mushrooms for one minute. Pour over mushrooms and let stand in refrigerator for 3 days — stir occasionally.

MARBLEHEAD TOMALLEY

¼ lb. lobster tomalley (liver)	2-3 tbls. ketchup
½ lb. cream cheese at room temperature	2 tbls. melted butter
	Worcestershire sauce to taste

Add tomalley to cream cheese, and mix until smooth. Add a few drops of Worcestershire, the ketchup, and the butter. Mix thoroughly. Add more ketchup and Worcestershire to taste. Mixture will be thin, but thickens when refrigerated. Prepare at least 3 hours before serving.

BACON-WRAPPED WATER CHESTNUTS

1 5-oz. can whole water chestnuts, drained	2 tbls. sugar
¼ cup soy sauce	slices of bacon

Put drained water chestnuts in a bowl and cover with soy sauce. Let stand 30 minutes. Remove chestnuts from bowl and roll each one in sugar. Cut bacon strips in half lengthwise. Wrap each chestnut with bacon and secure with toothpicks. Place on rack in a shallow pan, and bake in a hot (400°) oven about 20 minutes. Drain on paper towels. If a broiling method is preferred, place pan 5 inches below heat and broil about 8 minutes, turning once.

BACON-WRAPPED DATES

2 dozen pitted dates,   **slices of bacon**
  California type preferred

Wrap a quarter slice of bacon around each date; secure with a toothpick. Place on rack in shallow pan. Bake at 400° about 20 minutes.

CHICKEN LIVERS IN BACON

6 chicken livers   **6 slices of bacon**
2 tbls. prepared mustard   **¼ cup dry bread crumbs**

Wash chicken livers in cold water; remove any membrane and discolored spots; cut in half. Dip livers in mustard. Cut bacon strips in half crosswise. Wrap a piece of bacon around each liver piece, and secure with a toothpick. Bake in a 425° oven for 15 minutes.

EASY CHICKEN-LIVER MOUSSE

1½ lbs. chicken livers   **3 tbls. grated onions**
½ cup heavy cream   **2 tbls. cognac**
1½ tsps. salt   **½ tsp. freshly ground black pepper**

Wash livers thoroughly; remove any membrane and discolored spots. Cut in half. Cover with cold water; bring to a boil; cook over low heat 3 to 5 minutes until no pink remains. Drain well on paper towels. Purée in blender with the cream, or force through a sieve and add cream, mixing well. Stir in salt, pepper, onions, and cognac. Taste for seasoning. Pack into a crock or mold, and chill for at least 4 hours. Unmold on plate, decorate with parsley. Makes about 2 cups.

MAKE AHEADS AND FREEZE

Hot Cheese:
½ cup grated sharp cheddar
¼ tsp. prepared mustard

¼ tsp. Worcestershire sauce
Mayonnaise or salad dressing to bind

Crabmeat:
1½ cups flaked crabmeat
2 tbls. cream
1 hard-cooked egg, finely chopped

¼ cup salad dressing
salt and pepper to taste

Mushroom:
2 lbs. fresh mushrooms, chopped
   and sautéed

8 ozs. cream cheese
salt and pepper to taste

Avocado-Shrimp:
½ cup mashed avocado
½ cup chopped cooked shrimp

1 tbls. lemon juice
salad dressing to bind

Mix ingredients of each receipe in individual bowls. Toast one side of 1-inch bread rounds. Spread mixtures on untoasted sides of bread rounds. Put some of each kind on cookie sheets. Cover tightly with foil. Freeze. When ready to serve, remove foil and broil. Rounds thaw and brown in about 5 minutes.

DEVILED EGGS
ONE DOZEN ASSORTED

Hard-boil one dozen eggs. Shell; cut in half lengthwise; remove and mash (or rice) the yolks. Add any of the following variety of ingredients to the yolks for a pleasing assortment. Fill whites. Refrigerate until served.

1. Minced pimiento, parsley, dry mustard, and mayonnaise.
2. Butter, grated Roquefort, and paprika.
3. Tartar sauce and flaked seafood (shrimp, crab, or lobster).
4. Mashed avocado, lemon juice, and mayonnaise.
5. Sour cream and chopped almonds.
6. Ground ham, mustard, and mayonnaise.
7. Horseradish and mayonnaise; top with watercress sprig.
8. Celery seed, chopped olives, and French dressing.
9. Cream cheese, lemon juice, grated onion; topped with caviar.
10. Mayonnaise and curry powder.
11. Durkee dressing and hot-dog relish.
12. Mayonnaise and chopped crisp bacon.

NUGGETS

2 cups sharp Cheddar, grated
½ cup butter, softened
1 cup flour, sifted

1 tsp. paprika
salt to taste
pimiento-stuffed olives

Combine all ingredients, except olives, to form a dough. Blanket each large olive with 1 tablespoon of dough. Refrigerate or freeze. Bake nuggets on ungreased cookie sheet at 400° for 20 minutes or until golden. For variety, shape mixture around browned sausages or chunks of uncooked franks. For smaller nuggets, use 1 teaspoon of dough to cover small olives. Makes 4 dozen large nuggets; 6 dozen small.

BAKED CHEESE PUFFS

½ lb. Feta cheese, crumbled
½ lb. Swiss cheese, diced
3 eggs, slightly beaten
¼ cup chopped parsley

2 tbls. fine dry bread crumbs
1 lb. phyllo pastry
1½ cups butter or margarine,
  melted

Combine cheeses, eggs, parsley, and bread crumbs. Cut half the sheets of phyllo pastry into strips 3½ inches wide. Refrigerate the unused sheets and half the strips. Cover rest of strips with waxed paper and a damp towel to keep them from drying. Brush one strip with melted butter; top with a second strip and brush it with butter. Place one tablespoon of cheese mixture on top near one end; fold both strips of pastry over filling, forming a triangle; continue folding pastry triangle fashion, to end of strips. Repeat with remaining strips and cheese mixture. Place puffs on greased Jelly Roll pans; brush with melted butter. Bake at 350° for 20 minutes or until golden. Makes 70 puffs. Freeze well.

Soups

L. St. Clair

HOT TOMATO SURPRISE

2 cans tomato soup, undiluted	**1 tbls. prepared horseradish**
4 cans beef consommé, undiluted	

Mix soups and heat. When hot, add horseradish — more or less than one tablespoon to taste. Serves eight.

SPICY CLEAR TOMATO SOUP

1 onion	**2 tbls. sugar**
5-6 cloves	**3 beef bouillon cubes**
3 cups water or vegetable liquid	**1 bay leaf**
3-4 large tomatoes	**Pepper to taste**

Chop onion; cook until softened in enough water to cover. Peel, core, and chop tomatoes. Mix all ingredients and simmer until well blended. May be served as is or strained.

TOMATO SOUP

1 qt. tomatoes, peeled & quartered	**1 tbls. flour**
3 pts. water	**¼ cup butter, softened**
1 cup milk	**salt and pepper**

Rub flour into softened butter; add to tomatoes, water, and milk. Bring to a boil, and boil gently for ½ hour. Strain. Salt and pepper to taste.

CHINESE CHICKEN AND MUSHROOM SOUP

½ lb. uncooked chicken breasts
1 tsp. salt
1 tbls. cornstarch
3 tbls. cold water
1 tbls. soy sauce

4 cups chicken stock
4 large fresh mushrooms
  sliced thickly
½ tbls. peanut oil
2 tbls. lemon juice

Skin chicken breast meat and cut into cubes; sprinkle with ½ teaspoon of salt and let stand 30 minutes. Mix cornstarch with cold water; add to chicken stock with soy sauce and ½ teaspoon of salt; bring to boil. Simmer chicken cubes in stock mixture for 5 minutes. Sauté mushrooms in oil to soften, not brown. Add mushrooms and lemon juice to stock. Add additional salt to taste. Heat without boiling when ready to serve. Garnish each bowl with a thin slice of lemon.

PEASANT SOUP

1 lb. round steak, cut in
  ½" x 3" strips
1 large onion, sliced
1 1-lb. bag sauerkraut
2 stalks celery, chopped
2 apples, peeled and chopped
2 1-lb. cans of tomatoes

1 tsp. paprika
4 beef bouillon cubes
4 cups boiling water
1 bayleaf
1 tsp. caraway seeds
¼ cup sugar
salt and pepper to taste

Sauté beef strips with onion in Dutch oven until brown, using as little oil as possible to prevent sticking. Remove from pan and set aside. Add one cup of water to pan to loosen brown bits. Soften bouillon cubes in rest of water. Return meat and onions to pan. Add all other ingredients. Simmer, covered, for one hour.

CREAM OF ARTICHOKE SOUP

1 12-oz. can artichoke hearts
2 cups chicken broth
1 tbls. lemon juice

salt and pepper to taste
1 to 1½ cups light cream

Drain and thoroughly rinse artichokes; squeeze out excess water. Place artichokes in a blender with broth. Purée at high speed about ½ minute. Place in large saucepan with lemon juice, salt and pepper; bring to a boil; remove from heat. Stir in cream; reheat, but do **not** boil. Serves 4.

LEEK AND POTATO SOUP

1 bunch leeks	**3 chicken bouillon cubes**
6 cups boiling water	**2 medium-size potatoes**

Cut off and discard roots and green tops of leeks. Cut in 1-inch slices. Add to boiling water with bouillon cubes. Peel potatoes, dice, and add to soup. Cook until potatoes are soft. Mash; put through food mill or blender. Serve hot; or cold with a dollop of sour cream.

CORN CHOWDER

2 small onions, chopped	**1 17-oz. can cream-style corn**
1½ cups diced potato	**1 pt. coffee cream**
¾ cup water	**1 cup milk**

Pan fry onions in small amount of butter or oil until golden. Add diced potatoes and water; cook until potatoes are done. Add corn, cream, and milk. Bring to simmering point. Transfer to a double boiler off heat for at least one hour, half covered. Reheat to serve. Serves 6.

FRENCH SORREL SOUP

2 handfuls of French sorrel	**2 cups hot chicken stock**
4 tbls. butter	**2 egg yolks**
1 tsp. rice flour	**1 cup light cream**
salt and pepper to taste	**sour cream**

Wash and dry sorrel; chop fine and cook in butter until it becomes pulpy. Sprinkle with flour, salt, and pepper; mix well. Add hot chicken stock; simmer for 20 minutes. Pour into blender and blend on medium speed about 25 seconds. Cool. Beat egg yolks and cream together. Add to cooled mixture. (Adding while hot will cause eggs to curdle.) Reheat — do **not** boil — just before serving. Serve with dollop of sour cream.

THICK VEGETABLE SOUP — SAUDI ARABIA

1½ cups diced meat or chicken,
  cooked
1½ cups meat or chicken stock
1 tbls. chopped green pepper
1 tbls. chopped onion
1½ cups milk

4 cups shredded vegetables
  (cabbage, green beans, cauliflower,
  carrots, lima beans, etc.)
1 bay leaf
salt to taste

Combine meat, stock, bay leaf, and salt in kettle; bring to boil. Add vegetables. Cover and simmer 20 to 30 minutes until vegetables are tender. Add milk gradually. Cook stirring for 2 minutes. Serves 6.

BURT'S CHINESE "TOMATO" SOUP

4 10½-oz. cans rich chicken stock
6-8 dried black chinese mushrooms
  soaked, stemmed, and diced
3 fresh tomatoes, peeled, seeded
  and chopped
6 to 8 water chestnuts, rinsed, and
  finely diced
¼ lb. ground pork or beef

1 tsp. soy sauce
½ tsp. sugar
6 tbls. ketchup
2 tbls. cornstarch dissolved in 2 tbls.
  water
2 eggs, beaten
1 tsp. sesame oil

Pour stock into a large pot and add sugar, soy sauce, diced mushrooms, water chestnuts. Bring to boil, and add ground meat. Boil 3 minutes and add ketchup and diced tomatoes. Boil for 1 minute more. Lower heat until soup is simmering. Stir cornstarch mixture, and add to soup while stirring gently. Turn off heat and while stirring soup with a circular motion, slowly pour beaten egg into soup. Stir in sesame oil and serve. Serves 6 to 8.

CRAB SOUP

2 cups tomato soup
1 cup pea soup
1 cup cream
1 lb. crabmeat

1/3 cup sherry
1 cup beef bouillon
1 tbls. curry powder

Heat the tomato soup, then add the pea soup, and then the bouillon. When all are hot, turn into a double boiler. Add cream and crabmeat; heat until hot. Add curry and stir in well. Add sherry. Serve hot. Serves 6 to 8.

SEAFOOD BISQUE

1 can minced clams & juice
   (6½ ozs.)
½ lb. scallops, chopped (8 ozs.)
1 can lobster meat (8 ozs.)
1 can evaporated milk (13 ozs.)

3 cups milk
1-2 tbls. butter
salt and pepper to taste
Paprika

Put clams and juice in large pan, add scallops, and bring to a boil. Reduce heat; add lobster meat. Slowly add evaporated milk and milk. Add butter, salt, and pepper. Ladle into chowder bowls; sprinkle with paprika. Serves 4 to 6.

THICK SEAFOOD CHOWDER

4 slices bacon, diced
6 tbls. butter or margarine
2 cups chopped onion
3 cups cubed potatoes
2 lbs. seafood — any combination
   (ex. 1 lb. flounder, ½ lb. shrimp,
   and ½ lb. king crab)

3 6½-oz. cans minced clams with juice
2 cups fresh bread crumbs
2 13-oz. cans evaporated milk
2 bottles clam juice
3 cups milk

Cook bacon In very large kettle, add margarine, onions, and potatoes, and cook for 5 minutes. Add all remaining ingredients and bring to simmering point. Simmer — **do not boil** — for 2 hours. Add salt and pepper to taste before serving. The "secret" ingredient is the bread, which disappears in the cooking and provides the thickening agent. Freezes well after **one** hour of simmering. After defrosting, simmer for second hour. Serves 10 to 12.

NEW ENGLAND CLAM CHOWDER

1 pt. clams
1 medium onion, sliced
2 cups potatoes, sliced or diced
small piece of salt pork,
   diced (¼ cup)

2 cups milk, heated
1 can evaporated milk
1 cup clam juice, bottled
2 tbls. butter
salt and pepper to taste

Fry salt pork until golden brown; add onions and sautée until tender but not brown. Add clam juice, and bring to a boil. Add potatoes, and cook until just tender. Add clams. Stir in warm milk, and heat, but do **not** boil. Stir in evaporated milk. Salt and pepper to taste. Drop butter by spoonsfuls on top. Let stand 10-15 minutes for flavor to develop. Serve hot. Serves 2 to 4.

SCALLOP SOUP

1 qt. water
1 shallot, or 1 tbls. scallion,
   thinly sliced
¾ cup dry white wine
1/8 tsp. saffron (optional)
¾ cup cream

1½ tsp. salt
½ tsp. pepper
¼ tsp. dry mustard
1/8 tsp. curry powder
2 tbls. chopped chives or paprika
½ lb. scallops

In a non-aluminum pot, put water, wine, shallot, saffron, mustard, curry, salt, and pepper. Simmer, covered, for 15 minutes. Add scallops, cover, and simmer for 5 more minutes. Purée mixture in **blender**, one-half at a time. (Scallops do not purée completely, but remain in tiny pieces.) Return puréed mixture to pot; stir in cream, reheat, but do **not** boil. Ladle into serving dishes, spooning from bottom of pot to include scallop bits. Top with chives or paprika. Serves 2 to 4.

NEW ENGLAND FISH CHOWDER

1 lb. chowder fish in large chunks
   (cod or haddock)
2 cups potatoes, sliced or cubed
½ cup sliced onion (one medium)
small piece of salt pork, diced

2 cups milk, heated
1 can evaporated milk
3 tbls. butter
1½ cups boiling water
salt and pepper to taste

Fry out the salt pork until lightly brown. Add onions and cook until tender but not brown. Add boiling water and potatoes; cook, about 15 minutes, until potatoes are just tender. Add fish, and simmer about one minute. Add evaporated milk. Add heated milk. Salt and pepper to taste. Remove from heat. Drop butter by spoonfuls on top. Let stand at least 10 minutes for flavors to develop. Keep on low heat, and serve piping hot. (Four slices of cut-up bacon may be substituted for salt pork.)

LOBSTER BISQUE

3 lobster carcasses, chopped
4 - 6 tbls. butter
1 minced onion
1 cup finely chopped celery
1 bay leaf
½ tsp. Spanish paprika
1 lb. lobster meat in bite-size pieces

3 tbls. flour
2 cups chicken broth
2 cups milk
½ cup heavy cream
6 tbls. brandy or cognac
pinch of thyme
lobster coral and tomalley

Place lobster carcasses in a skillet with butter and paprika. Add lobster coral and tomalley if available. Add onion, celery, bay leaf, and thyme. Stir; when vegetables begin to wilt and shells to sizzle, stir in flour. Add brandy; add chicken broth. Bring to a low boil and simmer 15 to 20 minutes. Add milk slowly. Remove from heat; strain, pressing ingredients to obtain all possible liquid. Return to heat; add heavy cream; add lobster meat. Heat, but do **not** boil. Serves 4 to 6.

SHRIMP STEW

3 medium potatoes, sliced thin,
   cooked
2 medium onions, sliced thin,
   sautéed lightly
1 3-oz. pkg. cream cheese

1 pt. milk
1 large <u>can</u> shrimp
butter
salt and pepper to taste

Place potatoes, onions, and cream cheese in a large sauce pan with just enough water to cover; heat, stirring, until cheese is dissolved. In another pan, heat milk, add butter and seasonings to taste; add shrimp cut into pieces. Combine the two mixtures; heat, but do not boil. Let stand several hours for flavor to develop. Serves 2 to 4.

COLD TOMATO SOUP

2 cups tomato juice
1 cup V-8 juice
5 scallions, minced
2 tbls. lemon juice
3 tbls. tomato paste
1 cup sour cream
chopped parsley

grated rind of ½ lemon
pinch of oregano
pinch of powdered thyme
½ tsp. curry powder
salt, sugar, and freshly ground
   pepper to taste

Mix all ingredients except sour cream and parsley. Refrigerate at least one hour. Just before serving, stir in sour cream. Pour into individual bowls and sprinkle with parsley. Serves 4.

CURRY SOUP

¼ cup butter
1 large onion, finely chopped
1 28-oz. can tomatoes
1 tbls. (heaping) flour
1 tbls. curry powder

2 cups soup — green turtle, beef
 broth, or consommé
1 pt. all-purpose cream
½ pt. light cream
salt and pepper to taste

Sauté onion in 2 tablespoons of the butter until soft. Add entire contents of the can of tomatoes. Simmer one hour. Strain. Season to taste. Keep liquid hot. In a large kettle, melt 2 tablespoons of butter; add flour; cook, stirring, for 3 minutes. Add curry powder; mix well. Add 2 cups of broth slowly, stirring rapidly until blended. Add 1½ pints of cream slowly. Let come to a boil; season to taste. Add onion and tomato liquid to cream mixture. **Do not boil** or contents will curdle. If not served immediately, keep warm or reheat in double boiler. May also be served cold. May be frozen.

BLENDER CUKE COOLER

2 cucumbers, peeled, seeded,
 and diced
1 cup chopped onion
1 potato, peeled and diced
1 tbls. lemon and pepper seasoning
 (optional)

1 tbls. lemon juice
3 tbls. butter
1 tbls. tarragon
1 clove garlic (optional)
2 cups chicken bouillon

Melt butter in large saucepan; cook cucumbers and onion until soft. Add potato, seasonings, lemon juice, and half the bouillon. Cook approximately 15 minutes, until potato is tender. Put about one-quarter of mixture in blender; purée until smooth; add to second half of the bouillon. Purée rest of cucumber-potato mixture in small amounts, adding to bouillon. Refrigerate overnight to allow flavor to develop. For thicker soup, add a second potato. Tarragon may be omitted and fresh mint added as a garnish before serving. For extra-rich soup, stir in heavy cream to taste before serving.

COLD ZUCCHINI SOUP

6 small (3 large) zucchini	salt and pepper to taste
1 large onion (white or Spanish) sliced	1½ cups milk or cream
3 cups chicken broth	1½ tsp. curry powder (or to taste)

Cut zucchini into one-inch cubes; combine with sliced onion. Sprinkle with curry powder; stir to coat vegetables. Add to chicken broth in a large saucepan; simmer 45 minutes covered. Remove from heat; purée in a blender. In a large bowl, combine vegetable purée and milk or cream. Salt and pepper to taste. Refrigerate until very cold (about 4 hours). Sprinkle with chopped chives or croutons. Serves 6 to 8.

CHILLED RASPBERRY SOUP

3 10-oz. pkgs. frozen raspberries	¾ cup sugar (or less to taste)
3½ cups berry juice and water	1 cup sour cream
1 cup Rosé wine	pinch of salt

Thaw and strain raspberries; reserve juice. Add enough water to juice to make 3½ cups. Place berries in blender; blend at high speed for 20 to 30 seconds; strain, to remove any seeds, into large saucepan. Add water mixture, wine, salt, and sugar. Bring to a boil; simmer, covered, for 5 minutes. Cool; add sour cream, mixing thoroughly. Chill. May be garnished with sprigs of fresh mint or thin slices of lime. Serves 6.

COLD PEACH SOUP

3 large, ripe peaches	4 cloves
2 cups water	1 tbls. tapioca
¾ cup sugar	¾ cup dry white wine
lemon peel	whipped cream

Peel the peaches; remove stones; slice thinly. Combine water, sugar, cloves, and a dash of lemon peel in a large saucepan; bring to a boil; add tapioca; simmer 5 minutes; strain. Return syrup to saucepan; bring to simmering point; add peaches; stir in wine. When mixture reaches simmering point again, remove from heat. Chill thoroughly. Serve with a dollop of whipped cream. A few blueberries may be sprinkled over the cream as a garnish.

LUNCHEON AL FRESCO

In the formal garden a table is set with a lovely embroidered blue Italian cloth, Venetian glassware, and the Cantagli maiolica c. 1890 from Florence, Italy. A summer delight to welcome guests!

Luncheon on Terrace

Cold Zucchini Soup

Crabmeat Salad

Katie's Biscuits

Oranges George V

STRAWBERRY SOUP

1½ cups water
¾ cup light-bodied red wine
½ cup sugar
2 tbls. fresh lemon juice

1 stick cinnamon
1 qt. strawberries, stemmed and pureed
½ cup whipping cream
¼ cup sour cream

Combine water, wine, sugar, lemon juice, and cinnamon in a 3- to 4-quart saucepan. Boil uncovered for 15 minutes, stirring occasionally. Add strawberry purée and boil, stirring frequently, for 10 minutes more. Discard cinnamon stick and cool. Whip cream; combine with sour cream, and stir into strawberry mixture. Serve at cool room temperature.

EASY GAZPACHO

1 small green pepper, seeded and sliced
3 ripe tomatoes, peeled, seeded, and quartered
1 large cucumber, peeled, sliced and seeded
½ small onion, sliced
¼ tsp. freshly ground pepper

1 clove garlic
½ tsp. basil
1 tsp. salt
2 tbls. olive oil
3 tbls. wine vinegar
½ cup chicken broth chilled

Combine all ingredients in blender; blend until mixed but not smooth. Chill well before serving. Serve with bowls of chopped chives and croutons. Serves 4.

COLD MELON SOUP

6 cups coarsely chopped cantaloupe
6 cups coarsely chopped honeydew
4 cups orange juice
⅔ cup fresh lime juice

6 tbls. honey (or to taste)
4 cups Brut champagne or
    dry white wine
fresh mint leaves

Finely chop half of cantaloupe and honeydew; set aside, Puree remaining melon in batches with juices and honey in blender or processor. Pour into large bowl; stir in champagne and reserved melon. Cover and chill several hours. Garnish with fresh mint leaves. Serves 20.

CALDEREIDA (PORTUGESE FISH STEW)

2 lbs. peeled and sliced potatoes
4 medium onions, sliced thinly
4 tomatoes, peeled and sliced
4 lbs. mixed fish, cut in chunks
    (halibut, cod, octopus, shrimp
    clams, etc.)
1 to 2 cups water
1 cup white wine

5 cloves garlic, crushed
½ cup chopped parsley
1½ tsp. salt
2 bay leaves
½ cup olive oil
2 tbls. butter
¼ cup vinegar
pepper

In a 4-quart casserole, layer first the potatoes, then onions, tomatoes, and fish. Dot each layer with butter. Add wine and enough water to cover. Sprinkle with garlic, parsley, bay leaves, salt, and pepper. Pour olive oil over mixture. Bring to a boil; cover; simmer for 1 hour or more. Just before serving, stir in vinegar. Serves 6.

Salads

Lynn St.Clair

SPICE FRUIT MOLD

1 envelope gelatin
¼ cup water
1 tbls. mixed pickling spices
¼ cup sugar

2 tbls. lemon juice
1 cup seedless grapes
1 cup fresh blueberries
1¾ cups pineapple juice (canned)

In saucepan, soften gelatin in the cold water. Add pineapple juice, spices, sugar, and lemon juice. Bring to boil; cover and let stand for five minutes. Strain out spices. Refrigerate until partially set. Add fruit to gelatin mix; put into mold. Refrigerate until set. Unmold and serve with dressing made of ½ mayonnaise and ½ whipped cream.

MOLDED BING CHERRIES

1 lemon
2 envelopes plain gelatin
½ cup orange juice
1 cup sherry

1 large jar (or can) pitted Bing cherries, drained
1 cup orange juice

Soak gelatin in ½ cup orange juice. Add juice from drained cherries to one cup of orange juice and the sherry. Heat to boiling point; add gelatin, and stir until dissolved. Refrigerate until mixture begins to thicken; pour into a mold; add cherries. Chill until firm. Serves 6.

STRAWBERRY SALAD

2 pkgs. strawberry gelatin
1½ cups boiling water
2 8-oz. pkgs. frozen strawberries
(put in frozen)

1 large can crushed pineapple including juice
2 mashed bananas
1 pint sour cream

Mix all ingredients except sour cream. Put a layer in a mold or pan; when firm, cover with the sour cream, then the remaining gelatin mixture. Chill for 4 hours or overnight until firm.

GINGERALE SALAD

2 envelopes plain gelatin
¾ cup boiling water
2 cups gingerale
½ cup lemon juice
½ cup sugar
½ tsp. salt

1 cup canned pineapple chunks, drained
1 cup grapefruit sections, drained
1 cup Bing cherries, pitted and drained
1 cup seeded grapes, halved
½ cup chopped almonds

Dissolve gelatin in water; add lemon juice, sugar, salt, and gingerale. Set aside or in refrigerator until it begins to gel. Drain all juice from fruit; add to partially gelled mixtured. Mix well. Spoon into a mold which has been rinsed in cold water. Refrigerate until set.

LAYERED FRUIT SALAD

2 cups shredded iceberg lettuce
2 golden delicious apples
2 navel oranges
2 cups seedless green grapes, halved
2 tsps. lemon juice

1/3 cup mayonnaise
1/3 cup sour cream
1 cup shredded mild Cheddar or Swiss cheese

Spread lettuce on bottom of shallow two-quart serving dish. Core apples; slice thinly; sprinkle with lemon juice; layer over the lettuce. Peel and section oranges, removing all of white membrane; layer over apples. Spread grapes over oranges. Combine mayonnaise and sour cream; spread over fruit, "frosting" to completely cover. Sprinkle cheese over "frosting". Cover with plastic wrap. Refrigerate overnight. Cut in squares to serve. Makes 4 to 6 servings.

TWENTY-FOUR HOUR SALAD

2 17-oz. jars light or dark sweet cherries
1 11-oz. can mandarin orange segments
2 cups green grapes, seeded
2 cups minature marshmallows

2 eggs, slightly beaten
¼ cup frozen orange juice concentrate, thawed
¼ cup sugar
1 cup heavy cream, whipped

Drain cherries and oranges; combine with grapes and marshmallows. Combine eggs, orange concentrate, and sugar in top of a double boiler; cook over boiling water until thick and smooth. Cool. Fold in the whipped cream. Add dressing to fruit; mix well. Refrigerate 24 hours. Serves 8.

CRANBERRY-WINE MOLD

1½ cups cranberry juice
1 pkg. lemon-flavored gelatin
1 tsp. salt
1 cup port wine

1 cup red-skinned, chopped apple
 (cored)
½ cup chopped celery
¼ cup chopped nuts

Heat one cup of cranberry juice to boiling; remove from heat; stir in gelatin until dissolved. Add remaining cranberry juice and salt. Cool. Stir in port wine. Chill until partially set. Fold in apple, celery, and nuts. Pour into ring mold or individual molds. Chill until firm. Unmold on lettuce cups. Serves 6.

ELSA'S CRANBERRY SALAD

1 pkg. cherry gelatin
1 cup boiling water
1 can whole cranberry sauce

½ cup chopped celery
¼ cup chopped nuts
1 cup sour cream

Dissolve gelatin in boiling water; cool slightly. Break up the cranberry sauce and add to gelatin, mixing well. Add celery and nuts. Fold in sour cream. Spoon into a mold; refrigerate until set.

SIMPLE TOMATO ASPIC

2 pkgs. lemon gelatin
2 cups boiling water
2 8-oz. cans tomato sauce
2 tbls. vinegar
4 drops Tabasco

½ tsp. salt
½ tsp Lawry salt
¼ cup each chopped celery, onion,
 and green pepper

Dissolve gelatin in boiling water; add all ingredients except chopped vegetables. Put in refrigerator until mixture begins to gel. Stir in vegetables. Spoon into a ring mold. Refrigerate until firm.

CUCUMBER SALAD MOLD

1 pkg. lime gelatin
¾ cup hot water
1 cup chopped unpared cucumber
  (one medium size)

1 tsp. onion juice
¼ cup lemon juice
1 cup sour cream

Dissolve gelatin in hot water; add lemon and onion juices, chill until partially set. Stir in sour cream and cucumber. Chill till firm in mold. Serve with mayonnaise.

JELLIED MUSTARD RING

1 envelope plain gelatin
¼ cup water
4 eggs

¼ cup sugar
1½-3 tsps. dry mustard
1 cup heavy cream, whipped

Soak gelatin in water. Beat eggs until foamy; add sugar; add dry mustard through a sieve. Cook over hot water, stirring constantly, until mixture coats a spoon. Add gelatin, mixing well. Cool. When cool and beginning to thicken, fold in whipped cream. Spoon into a ring mold which has been rinsed with cold water. Chill until firm. Center may be filled with cole slaw.

AMY'S HORSERADISH MOLD

1 small box lemon or lime gelatin
1 cup boiling water
2 tbls. lemon juice
2/3 cup horseradish (drained)

¼ tsp. salt
1 cup heavy cream whipped
green food coloring (optional)

Dissolve gelatin in boiling water, cool until slightly thickened. Add lemon juice, horseradish, and salt. Fold in whipped cream. Fills a 4-cup mold. Chill.

COBB SALAD

1 medium head iceberg lettuce,
  broken coarsely
2 cups watercress leaves,
  coarsely chopped
½ lb. bacon, crisply cooked
  and crumbled

2 medium-sized avocados, peeled,
  pitted, and sliced
2½ cups cut-up, cooked chicken
  breasts
1 tbls. minced chives
3 hard-cooked eggs, quartered

Combine all ingredients, toss lightly. Line one large or 6 individual salad bowls with crisp greens. Add salad mixture. Serve with creamy French dressing. Serves 6 to 8.

REUBEN SALAD

1 12-oz. can corned beef, chilled
1 head lettuce, broken up
1 cup sauerkraut, rinsed and
  well drained
2 cups cubed Swiss cheese

5 slices rye bread
1 cup Thousand Island dressing
½ tsp. caraway seeds (optional)
butter or margarine

Trim crusts from bread; spread both sides with butter. Cut slices into ½-inch cubes. Spread on baking sheet; bake in 300° oven for approximately 30 minutes. Slice corned beef into julienne strips; combine with lettuce, sauerkraut, cheese, and rye bread croutons in large salad bowl. Combine dressing and caraway seeds; pour over salad mixture, serve at once. Serves 8. Salad may be refrigerated several hours with dressing added just before serving.

FATTOUSH (MIXED SALAD SAUDI ARABIA)

3 tomatoes, peeled and diced
2 cucumbers, peeled and diced
1 green pepper, chopped fine
8 scallions, sliced thin
4 tbls. parsley, chopped fine

½ cup olive oil
¼ cup lemon juice
1 tsp. salt
2 cups croutons (optional)
4 sprigs fresh mint, chopped fine

Combine in large bowl and toss gently the tomatoes, cucumbers, green pepper, scallions, parsley, and mint. This may be done ahead, covered, and refrigerated. One hour before serving, combine olive oil, lemon juice, and salt. Add to vegetables and toss lightly. Croutons may be added just before serving. The secret of this salad is the finely chopped vegetables. Serves 6.

SPINACH SALAD

2 lbs. fresh spinach, crisped
1 lb. fresh bean sprouts, crisped
2 small (4 oz. total) red onions,
   thinly sliced

8 large (½ lb. total) mushrooms,
   sliced
2 hard-cooked eggs, halved lengthwise
6 slices crisply cooked bacon, crumbled

Line shallow salad bowl with some whole spinach leaves. Tear remaining leaves into bite-size pieces and add to bowl. Top with bean sprouts. Arrange onion rings over top; add mushrooms. Carefully separate egg whites from yolks. Chop whites coarsely. Finely chop or rice the yolks. Arrange whites and yolks separately in concentric circles in center of salad. Place crumbled bacon in middle. Chill. At serving time, add Hot Salad Dressing (see dressings) and toss gently.

SOUTH SEA SALAD

½ cup mayonnaise or salad dressing
½ cup sour cream
¼ cup dill pickle juice
½ avocado, mashed
1 tbls. snipped parsley
2 tsps. snipped chives
1 tsp. dried dillweed

1 bunch red-tipped leaf lettuce, torn
1 11-oz. can mandarin oranges, drained
1 cup fresh mushrooms, sliced
1 small onion, sliced and separated
   into rings
1 green pepper, sliced in rings
½ avocado, sliced

Combine mayonnaise, sour cream, pickle juice, mashed avocado, parsley, chives and dillweed. Cover and refrigerate. Place lettuce in large bowl. Arrange oranges, mushrooms, onion, green pepper, and sliced avocado attractively on top of lettuce. Toss salad with desired amount of dressing just before serving. Serves 4 to 6.

CURRIED VEGETABLE SALAD

1 16-oz. pkg. frozen green beans,
   cauliflower, and carrots*
salt and pepper

2 tbls. curry powder
4 tbls. mayonnaise
lettuce

Cook vegetables until crisply tender in salted water to which one tablespoon of curry powder has been added. Drain in sieve, and run cold water over vegetables to stop cooking. Chill in refrigerator. Mix second tablespoon of curry powder with mayonnaise; add to vegetables just before serving. Add salt and pepper to taste. Serve on lettuce. Serves 4 to 5.
*Other combinations may be used.

ARTICHOKE-RICE SALAD

1 pkg. chicken-flavored rice mix
4 green onions, sliced
½ green pepper, chopped
12 pimiento-stuffed olives, sliced

2 6-oz. jars marinated artichoke hearts
¾ tsp. curry powder
⅓ cup mayonnaise

Cook rice as directed on package, omitting butter. Cool; add onions, pepper, and olives. Drain artichokes, reserving marinade. Cut artichokes in half (or smaller if preferred). Combine marinade with curry powder and mayonnaise. Add hearts to rice, and toss with the dressing. Chill. Serves 8.

FIRE AND ICE TOMATOES

6 large ripe tomatoes
1 or 2 large cucumbers
1 or 2 large green peppers
2 red onions
¾ cup vinegar
¼ tsp. black pepper

1½ tsps. celery salt
4½ tsps. sugar
¼ tsp. mustard seed
½ tsp. salt
½ tsp red (cayenne) pepper

Quarter tomatoes; slice peppers into rounds, onions into rings. Put all into a large bowl. Boil all seasonings and vinegar furiously for 1 minute. Pour over vegetables while still hot. Chill thoroughly. Just before serving add sliced and peeled cucumbers.

LAYERED SALAD

1 head iceberg lettuce
1 large sweet onion, sliced thin
1 head cauliflower
1 lb. bacon, cooked and crumbled

1 pt. real mayonnaise
2 tbls. sugar
1 cup Parmesan cheese
grated Cheddar cheese

Break up lettuce in bowl; cover with onion slices. Break cauliflower into flowerets; slice flowerets; place over onion. Sprinkle bacon over cauliflower. Spread real mayonnaise over all. Sprinkle the two tablespoons of sugar over the mayonnaise. Sprinkle this with Parmesan cheese. Grate enough Cheddar to completely cover all. Cover tightly with plastic wrap, and refrigerate overnight. Toss before serving. Serves 6 to 8.

TWENTY-FOUR HOUR SALAD

1 small head iceberg lettuce,
  shredded
1 pkg. fresh spinach, crisped
  and shredded
2 hard-cooked eggs, sliced
1 medium onion, sliced very thin
½ lb. bacon, crisply cooked
  and crumbled

1 cup frozen tiny peas, thawed,
  but uncooked
1 cup sour cream
1 cup real mayonnaise
1 tbls. lemon juice
1 tbls. Worcestershire
shredded Swiss cheese

Layer first six ingredients in glass salad bowl or rectangular dish. Mix next four ingredients; spread over vegetables like a frosting. Sprinkle cheese on top. Refrigerate overnight. Serves 8 to 10.

THREE-STEP SLAW

4 lbs. cabbage shredded finely
1 green pepper cut in thin rings
1 large onion cut in thin rings
2 cups sugar

1 cup vinegar
1 cup vegetable oil
1 tsp. salt
1½ tsps. celery seed

Toss vegetables lightly with sugar and let stand while dressing is prepared. Mix oil, vinegar, celery seed, and salt in pan. Bring to boil. Remove from heat. While hot pour over vegetables and toss. May be kept in refrigerator up to three weeks. Serves 6 to 10.

MARINADE FOR TOMATOES

½ tsp. sugar
¾ tsp. salt
¼ tsp. pepper
½ tsp. oregano
½ tsp. dried basil

3 tbls. oil
2 tbls. wine vinegar
¼ tsp. garlic salt
sliced onions and tomatoes

Mix all ingredients except onions and tomatoes; pour over the onions and tomatoes. Refrigerate several hours.

CREAMY FRENCH DRESSING

⅔ cup salad oil
⅓ cup vinegar
¼ cup ketchup
½ tsp. dry mustard
½ tsp. paprika

¼ tsp. Tabasco
1/8 tsp. salt
½ tsp. sugar
2 tbls. blue cheese, crumbled

Combine all ingredients in covered jar. Shake well, and store in refrigerator. Shake well again before using. Makes 1¼ cups.

POPPY SEED DRESSING (1)

¼ cup sugar
1 tsp. dry mustard
1 tsp. salt

⅓ cup vinegar
1 cup vegetable oil
1½ tbls. poppy seeds

Combine sugar, mustard, salt, and vinegar in a blender. Gradually add the oil until a creamy consistency forms. Add the poppy seeds and blend 2-3 minutes longer. Refrigerate until ready to serve.

POPPY SEED DRESSING (2)

2 cups sugar
2 tbls. dry mustard
2 tsps. salt
½ grated onion

1 cup white vinegar
4 cups cottonseed oil
3 tbls. poppy seeds

Mix together the sugar, dry mustard, salt, and grated onion. Add vinegar and mix well. Add oil slowly, stirring constantly. Add poppy seeds and mix.

SWEET SALAD DRESSING

1 tsp. salt

1 tsp. dry mustard

1 tsp. sugar

1 tsp. paprika

½ tsp. cayenne pepper

2 tbls. tomato ketchup

1 cup oil

¼ cup vinegar

Mix together in bottle. Store in refrigerator. Serve with fruit salads.

TOMATO SAUCE SALAD DRESSING

1 cup oil

1 can tomato soup

⅔ cup cider vinegar

½ cup sugar

1 small lemon (juiced) or
   ¼ cup lemon juice

1 tbls. salt

1 tbls. Worcestershire sauce

1 small onion, grated

1 clove garlic

Mix all ingredients well. Bottle and store in refrigerator. Serve on salad greens.

HOT SALAD DRESSING

⅔ cup safflower oil

¼ cup cider vinegar

¼ cup ketchup

1 to 3 tbls. honey

1 tsp. sesame oil

1 tsp. dry mustard

1 tsp. celery seed

1 tsp. celery salt

½ tsp. salt

Combine all ingredients and mix well. Transfer to small saucepan. At serving time, place over low heat until very warm; do **not** boil. Makes approximately 1½ cups.

CHARTER HOUSE DRESSING

1 egg
¼ tsp. garlic powder
¼ tsp. chopped anchovies
1 pinch onion powder
1 pinch paprika
1 pinch dry mustard
½ cup wine vinegar

¼ tsp. freshly ground pepper
1 tbls. lemon juice
1 cup olive oil
4 cups salad oil
¼ tsp. salt
1 pinch sugar

Mix thoroughly all spices, salt, sugar, and anchovies. Beat egg until foamy; add spice mixture. Continue to beat, slowly adding the olive oil and the lemon juice. Add the salad oil and the wine vinegar alternately. While pouring the oil, be sure mixture does not get too thick or it will break down. Strain. May be refrigerated.

STRAWBERRY SALAD DRESSING

1 8-oz. container whipped
    "topping"
1 tbls. mayonnaise

1 tbls. lemon juice
1 1-lb. pkg. frozen strawberries

Thaw the strawberries. Fold mayonnaise and lemon juice into whipped topping. Fold in the thawed berries. Good served with fruit gelatins.

Breads

L. St. Clair

BRAN MUFFINS

1½ cups bran
1 cup stone ground whole wheat
   flour
¼ cup wheat germ
3 tsps. baking powder
dash powdered cinnamon

½ cup blond raisins
½ cup dark molasses
2 tbls. oil
¾ cup milk
1 egg

Mix dry ingredients; add raisins which have been plumped by steaming. Add molasses, oil, milk, and egg beaten with a fork. Mix all together thoroughly. Spoon into muffin pans lined with paper cups. Bake in a preheated oven at 375° for 15-18 minutes. Freezes well. Makes 12.

BANANA BRAN MUIFFINS

1 cup sifted flour
½ tsp. salt
¾ tsp. soda
2 tbls. shortening
2 tbls. sour milk or buttermilk

2 cups thinly sliced banana
¼ cup sugar
1 egg, well beaten
1 cup All-Bran

Sift together the flour, salt, and soda. Rub the shortening to a creamy consistency with the back of a spoon. Stir the sugar slowly into the shortening till mixture is light and fluffy. Add egg, bran, and milk. Blend thoroughly and let stand while slicing the bananas. Add bananas to mixture and blend well. Stir in dry ingredients, mixing only to dampen all the flour. Bake in well greased muffin tins in a 375° oven — small tins, 15-20 minutes; large tins — 25-30 minutes (Note: if bran package has been previously opened, an extra tablespoon of milk may be necessary.)

CARROT-RAISIN MUFFINS

2 cups sugar
1¼ cups oil
4 eggs, lightly beaten
3 cups flour
2 tsps. baking powder

1 tsp. baking soda
1 dash salt
2 cups grated carrots
½ cup chopped nuts
½ cup raisins

Beat sugar and oil together in medium bowl; blend in the eggs. Combine flour, baking powder, soda, and salt. Slowly stir into oil mixture, blending thoroughly. Add carrots, nuts, and raisins. Spoon into greased muffin tins until two-thirds full. Bake at 350° for 35 to 40 minutes. Makes 30 muffins.

VICTORIAN PICNIC

A loaf of bread, a jug of wine, and pretty ladies in print gowns set the scene for a "simple" Victorian picnic. To be proper, tables, chairs, china, and glassware all must be transported to the site of the repast.

Picnic

Devilled Eggs

Cold Tomato Soup

Chicken   *Ham*

Layered Salad

Banbury Tarts

Fruit   *Cheese*

Wine

OATMEAL MUFFINS

1 cup flour	1⅓ cups quick-cooking oatmeal
¼ cup sugar	1 cup buttermilk
1½ tsps. baking powder	¼ cup molasses
½ tsp. soda	¼ cup oil
salt to taste	1 egg

Mix together all dry ingredients in large bowl. Beat together the egg, buttermilk, oil, and molasses. Add to dry ingredients and stir just until mixed. Pour into muffin tins (12 muffins) and bake in a 400° oven for 25 minutes. These muffins will be flat.

CHESTNUT MUFFINS

1½ cups sifted flour	3 tbls. sugar
½ cup sifted chestnut flour*	1 egg, well beaten
½ tsp. salt	1 cup milk
1 cup chestnuts, broken into small pieces**	3 tbls. melted butter

Mix and sift together the dry ingredients. Combine egg, milk, and butter; add to flour mixture; stir until just combined. Fill greased muffin tins ⅔ full. Bake at 425° for 20-30 minutes, depending on size of tins. Yields 12 to 15 muffins.
  *Chestnut flour may be obtained in Italian grocery shops.
**Chestnuts may be fresh, packed in water, or packed in syrup. If latter are used, rinse thoroughly before adding.

MARCIA'S BLUEBERRY MUFFINS

½ cup butter	½ cup milk
1½ cups sugar	½ tsp. salt
2 cups flour	2 tsps. baking powder
2 eggs	2½ cups blueberries

Set aside 2 tsps. of sugar for topping. Cream butter and sugar until light and fluffy. Beat in the 2 eggs. Sift together the dry ingredients; add to egg mixture alternately with the milk. Mash one cup of berries and stir into mixture; fold in the remaining berries. Grease muffin tins well, including top area of pan. Fill tins almost to top; sprinkle with set-aside sugar. Bake at 375° for 25 to 30 minutes. Cool in tins for ½ hour.

PUBLICK HOUSE PUMPKIN MUFFINS

2 cups sugar
½ cup vegetable oil
3 eggs
1½ cups pumpkin
½ cup water
3 cups flour
1½ tsps. baking powder

1 tsp. baking soda
½ tsp. cloves
¾ tsp. cinnamon
½ tsp. nutmeg
1 tsp. salt
1½ cups raisins
1 cup walnuts

Place sugar, oil, eggs, pumpkin and water in bowl and mix. Sift flour, baking powder, soda, salt and spices. Add to first mixture and mix. Add raisins and walnuts. Place in greased muffin pans and bake at 400° about 15 minutes. Makes 2 dozen.

COLD-OVEN POPOVERS

2 eggs, slightly beaten
1 cup milk
1 tbls. melted butter

½ tsp. salt
1 cup flour

Mix all ingredients and beat well for 4 minutes. Pour into greased custard cups or muffin tins. Refrigerate for several hours or overnight. Place in a cold oven. Bake at 400° for one hour. Do **not** open oven door while baking. Makes 6 popovers.

VARIATIONS ON A THEME
A BASIC MIXTURE

2 cups flour
½ cup sugar
1 tbls. baking powder
1 tsp. salt

1 egg, lightly beaten
¾ cup milk
⅓ cup vegetable oil

Mix flour, sugar, baking powder, and salt. In another bowl, mix egg, milk, and oil. With a spoon, make a well in the center of the flour mixture; pour in egg mixture; stir until all flour is moistened. Mixture may be lumpy.

BLUEBERRY MUFFINS

basic mixture   ½ cup butter, melted
1 cup fresh or frozen blueberries   ½ cup sugar

Add blueberries to the flour mixture with the beaten egg. Spoon into well-greased muffin tins. Bake at 400° for 20 to 22 minutes. Remove immediately from pan. Dip muffin tops into melted butter and then into sugar. Makes 12 muffins.

APPLE-CINNAMON MUFFINS

basic mixture   2 tbls. brown sugar
1 cup grated apple   2 tbls. flour
¼ cup golden raisins   ¼ tsp. cinnamon
½ tsp. cinnamon   1 tbls. butter

Add apple, raisins, and ½ tsp. cinnamon to flour mixture with the beaten egg. Combine brown sugar, 2 tbls. flour, and ¼ tsp. cinnamon; cut in butter until mixture is crumbly. Spoon batter into well-greased muffin tins. Sprinkle with brown sugar mixture. Bake at 400° for 20 to 22 minutes.

CRANBERRY-ORANGE MUFFINS

basic mixture   ¼ cup sugar
1 cup chopped cranberries   1 tsp. grated orange peel

Mix cranberries, sugar, and orange peel. Stir into flour mixture with beaten egg. Spoon into well-greased muffin tins. Bake at 400° for 20 to 22 minutes.

DATE-NUT MUFFINS

basic mixture   ½ cup chopped nuts
¾ cup chopped, pitted dates

Combine nuts and dates; stir into flour mixture, coating and separating date pieces. Add egg mixture. Spoon into well-greased muffin tins. Bake at 400° for 20 to 22 minutes.

To make miniature muffins, bake at 400° for 6 to 8 minutes.

CRANBERRY-SWIRL COFFEE CAKE

¼ lb. margarine
1 cup sugar
2 eggs
1 tsp. soda
2 cups all-purpose flour
½ tsp. salt

½ pt. (1 cup) sour cream
1 tsp. vanilla
½ cup nuts, chopped
7- or 8-oz. can whole-berry
    cranberry sauce

Cream margarine and sugar; add unbeaten eggs, one at a time, beating after each one (medium speed of electric mixer). Mix together the dry ingredients; add to egg mixture alternately with sour cream; add vanilla. Grease an 8- or 9-inch tube pan. Spoon one-third of batter on bottom; cover with half the cranberry sauce. Cover with one-half the nuts. Add one-third of batter; cover with cranberry sauce and nuts. Add remaining batter. Swirl batter into sauce and nuts with knife. Bake in 350° oven for 55 minutes or until cake tests done with a toothpick. Cool in pan for 5 minutes; turn out on rack to cool. May be frozen when cool.

APPLE COFFEE CAKE

5 tbls. sugar
2 tsps. cinnamon
3 cups flour, sifted once
1 cup sugar
1 cup cooking oil
4 eggs

¼ cup orange juice
2½ tsps. vanilla
3 tsps. baking powder
1 tsp. salt
3 large apples, peeled, cored, and
    thinly sliced

Combine 5 tablespoons of sugar with cinnamon; set aside. Combine flour, cup of sugar, oil, eggs, juice, vanilla, baking powder, and salt; beat well. Grease an 8- or 10-inch tube pan. Pour in one-third of batter; cover with one-half of the apple slices; sprinkle with one-half of the cinnamon mixture. Pour in second one-third of batter; cover with rest of apple slices and remaining cinnamon mixture. Pour in last one-third of batter. Bake at 350° for one hour and 10 minutes. Let cool completely before cutting or cake will crumble.

PENNSYLVANIA DUTCH COFFEE CAKE

1 egg
sour cream
1 cup sugar
1½ cups flour (scant)
cinnamon

1½ tsps. baking powder
large pinch of salt
butter
½ cup brown sugar

Break egg in measuring cup and fill cup with sour cream. Mix sugar, flour, baking powder and salt. Stir wet and dry ingredients together until no longer lumpy. Put mixture in deep 9″ pie plate and dot generously with butter. Cover with brown sugar (at least ½ cup) and sprinkle cinnamon over all. Bake in 350° oven 20 to 30 minutes. Freezes well.

CHEESE BISCUITS

1½ cups flour
2 tsps. baking powder
¼ tsp. salt

1 tbls. shortening
½ cup sharp Cheddar cheese, grated
1 scant cup milk

Sift flour, baking powder and salt together three times. Add shortening and the cheese, mixing in lightly or chopping in with knife. Add milk, just enough to hold mixture together. Roll out on floured board to ½ inch thickness; cut with small biscuit cutter. Brush over the top with sweet milk and place in buttered pans. Bake in hot oven 12 to 15 minutes — 400°.

KATIE'S BISCUITS

2 cups milk
2 yeast cakes
2 cups bread flour
½ cup melted butter

2 eggs, well beaten
1 tsp. salt
1 cup sugar
3-3½ cups flour

Scald milk; remove from heat and cool until lukewarm; add yeast and 2 cups of bread flour; stir to mix well. Let rise for one hour; if full of holes, beat down with a wooden spoon. Add melted butter, eggs, salt, and sugar; add 3 to 3½ cups flour; let rise for 2 to 3 hours; beat down with spoon. Roll out on lightly floured board; cut with circular cookie cutter; place in a buttered pan. Bake at 450° for about ½ hour. Brush over tops with a little melted butter as biscuits are removed from oven.

HAWTHORNE'S SOUR CREAM JOHNNYCAKE

¾ cup flour
¾ cup cornmeal (preferably yellow
    and stone ground)
¼ cup sugar
1 tbls. double-acting baking powder

½ tsp. salt
¼ tsp. soda
1 egg
1 cup sour cream

Combine all ingredients. Stir batter until smooth. Bake in a buttered 8-inch square pan in a pre-heated oven 400° for 20 minutes or until a cake-tester inserted in center comes out clean.

WHITE BREAD

2 cups scalded milk
1 tbls. - heaping - shortening
2 tbls. salt
2 tbls. sugar (or honey)
1 cup water

1 pkg. yeast
½ cup warm water
1 tsp. sugar
6-7 cups flour sifted (may use 1 cup
    of graham flour)

Scald milk; cool by adding one cup of water; add shortening to melt. Proof yeast in one-half cup of warm water (test one drop on wrist); add sugar; set aside to rise in cup. Put one cup of flour in a large bowl; add milk, sugar, and salt separately; add yeast; beat after each addition. Add flour a cup at a time until mixture becomes sticky. Turn out on a floured board; knead until smooth and elastic. Put into a greased bowl, cover; let rise in warm place. When double in size, knead down vigorously. Let rise again and reknead. Form into 3 loaves, and let rise again. Bake in 350° oven until loaves sound hollow when patted (about one hour).

"7-UP" DATE BREAD

1 cup chopped dates
7-oz. "7-up"
1 tsp. baking soda
1 cup sugar
2 tbls. margarine

1 egg
1½ cups flour
1 tsp. vanilla
pinch of salt

Add dates to "7-up" and bring to boil; add baking soda, stir, and set aside to cool. When cool, add remaining ingredients in following order: sugar, margarine, egg, salt, flour, and vanilla, stirring after each addition. Beat thoroughly by hand. Divide into 3 small, greased loaf pans and bake in 350° oven 35 to 40 minutes; or use 5 round soup cans, greased, and bake for 30 minutes.

SWISS CHEESE BREAD

1 can (12 oz.) beer or	2 tbls. butter or margarine
1½ cups milk	1 pkg. (8 ozs.) pasteurized process
½ cup warm water	Swiss or American cheese, diced
2 tbls. sugar	5 cups all-purpose flour
1 tbls. salt	2 pkgs. active dry yeast

Generously grease bottom and sides of two 9- x 5-inch loaf pans. In large saucepan, warm beer, water, sugar, salt, butter, and cheese. Cheese will soften but not melt. Cool to lukewarm. In large mixer bowl, combine 2 cups flour with yeast, add warm (not hot) cheese mixture. Beat 3 minutes at medium speed. By hand gradually stir in remaining 3 cups of flour to make a fairly stiff dough. Knead on lightly floured surface until smooth and elastic, about 5 minutes. Place in greased bowl, turning to grease top. Cover; let rise in warm place until double in size. Punch down dough; divide in half and shape into two 11- x 5-inch rectangles. Cut each rectangle into 3 long strips, leaving strips joined at one end. Braid. Place in prepared pans. Cover; let rise in warm place until light and double in size — 45 to 60 minutes. Bake at 350° for 40 to 45 minutes until deep golden brown and loaf sounds hollow when lightly tapped. Remove from pan immediately; cool completely. Makes 2 loaves.

LEMON BREAD

½ cup shortening	1½ cups flour
1½ cups sugar	1 tsp. baking powder
2 eggs, beaten	½ tsp. salt
½ cup milk	1 lemon — juice and grated rind

Cream together the shortening and one cup of the sugar; add eggs. Sift together the flour, baking powder, and salt; add to egg mixture alternately with the milk. Grate rind of lemon; add to the mixture. Bake in loaf pan in 350° oven for 45 minutes. Mix lemon juice with ½ cup of sugar. Pour over bread while still hot.

FINNISH COFFEE BREAD

2 pkgs. dried yeast
2 cups lukewarm milk
3 medium eggs
1 cup sugar
Coffee; sugar; melted butter

½ tsp. salt
½ tsp. crushed cardamon seed
  (husks removed)
4-6 cups all-purpose flour

Dissolve yeast in lukewarm milk. Beat eggs and add to yeast and milk. Add sugar, salt, and cardamon. Add flour gradually, using just enough so that mixture does not stick to a wooden spoon. Cover; let rise to double in bulk. Punch down, and divide in half. Braid each half, and let rise again. Brush each loaf with melted butter. Bake each loaf on a floured and greased cookie sheet for 25-30 minutes at 350°. Brush top and sides with hot coffee and sprinkle with granulated sugar.

BROWN BREAD

½ cup cornmeal
½ cup white flour
½ cup whole wheat flour

½ cup raisins
1 cup buttermilk
¼ cup molasses

Combine cornmeal with the two flours; add raisins, toss lightly until well coated. Mix buttermilk with molasses; add to dry ingredients. Mix lightly until well blended. Pour batter into well greased pudding mold. Cover, and place on rack in deep kettle. Add boiling water to cover ¾ of mold. Cover kettle. Steam approximately 2 hours. Remove from mold. Slice.

IRISH TEA BREAD

4 cups flour
3 tsps. baking powder
½ cup sugar
¼ tsp. salt
1 tbls. shortening
1 tbls. sugar (for topping)

½ cup raisins
½ cup currants
1 tbls. carraway seeds
2 cups milk
1 egg

Sift together the flour, baking powder, sugar, and salt; cut in the shortening. Add raisins, currants, and carraway seeds. Mix. Beat egg and milk together and add to mixture. Pour into greased, deep 10″ or 12″ loaf pan or 10″ round (2½ qt.) casserole. Sprinkle top with sugar; bake one hour at 350°. Cool for one hour before slicing. Currants and raisins may be soaked in ¼ cup of whiskey overnight for added flavor. May be frozen.

NOVA SCOTIA BREAD

1 cup oatmeal	4 cups water
1⁄3 - 1⁄2 cup cornmeal	2 yeast cakes dissolved in 1 cup water
6 tbls. shortening	1 1⁄3 cups molasses
1 tbls. salt	12 to 15 cups flour

Combine oatmeal, cornmeal, shortening, salt, water in a double boiler, stirring occasionally, until a porridge is made. Cool; place in a bread mixer. Combine yeast with one cup of warm water; add to porridge. Add molasses. Add flour until dough is clean from sides of mixer. Knead. Return to mixer bowl and let rise until double in size. Punch down. Form into 4 loaves; place in well greased loaf pans. Raise in warm place. Brush tops of loaves with melted butter. Bake at 375° for 45 to 50 minutes.

GEORGIA TEA BREAD

2 cups sugar	2 tsps. baking powder
1⁄2 cup butter or margarine	2 tsps. baking soda
2 eggs, slightly beaten	1 tsp. salt
grated rind of 2 oranges	1⁄2 tsp. cinnamon
grated rind of 1 lemon	1 1⁄2 cups orange juice
grated rind of 1 lime	1 cup jasmine tea
6 cups flour	1 cup chopped pecans

Combine sugar and butter until light; add eggs and grated rinds. Sift together the flour, baking powder, baking soda, salt and cinnamon. Combine orange juice and tea. Add to butter mixture alternately with flour mixture, beating well after each addition. Add nuts and combine well. Spoon batter into 2 well greased 9″ x 5″ x 3″ pans. Bake the loaves at 350° approximately one hour or until skewer inserted in middle comes out clean. Cool bread in pans for 10 minutes; turn out on wire rack. Freezes well.

ANADAMA BREAD

½ cup cornmeal
2 cups boiling water
2 tbls. shortening
½ cup molasses

2 tsps. salt
2 yeast cakes
½ cup lukewarm water
4 to 5 cups flour

Stir cornmeal into boiling water; add shortening, molasses, and salt. Add yeast cakes to lukewarm water to soften. Remove cornmeal mixture from heat; cool until lukewarm; stir in the softened yeast. Add enough flour to make a dough you can knead. Place in a greased bowl; let rise until double in bulk. Punch dough down; let rise again for approximately 45 minutes. Turn out on floured board; knead well. Shape into 2 loaves; place in greased bread tins; let rise until very light. Bake at 425° for 15 minutes; then at 375° for 45 minutes more. Remove loaves from oven; brush tops with melted butter while loaves are hot; set on rack to cool.

GERMAN PANCAKE

6 tbls. butter
6 eggs
1 cup milk

1 cup flour
1 tbls. salt

Preheat oven to 425°. Melt butter over low heat in a 9″ x 12″ or 9″ x 13″ pan. In a large bowl using an electric mixer (or in a blender), mix together the eggs, milk, flour, and salt thoroughly. Pour batter into melted butter in hot pan; do **not** stir. Place in oven immediately. Bake 15 to 20 minutes until crisp and golden brown. The butter and oven **must** be hot when batter put into oven. For half the recipe, use a 9″-square pan. For one-third, use an 8″-square pan.

RAISED WAFFLES

1 pkg. dry yeast
½ cup warm water
2 cups warm milk
½ cup oil
½ tsp. soda

1 tsp. salt
1 tsp. sugar
2 cups flour
2 eggs

Dissolve yeast in warm water. Add milk, oil, salt, sugar, and flour. Beat; cover; let stand at room temperature overnight. Next morning, beat in the eggs and soda. Bake in waffle iron. Makes 4. Serve with butter and maple syrup.

Entrées

KIPPERED HERRING IN CREAM

1 large onion
2 tbls. butter
1 can kippered herring

½ cup cream
Paprika

Slice onion and cook rings slowly in butter until soft and yellow. Remove from pan and put to side. Drain herring thoroughly and place fillets in residue in pan. Add cream and over low heat warm thoroughly. Remove to serving dish; garnish with cooked onions and sprinkle with paprika. Serve with toast triangles. One can makes 2 servings.

FINNISH HERRING SALAD

1 jar (8-oz.) pickled herring,
  chopped
1½ cups diced cooked potatoes
1 cup diced cooked beets
1 cup diced cooked carrots
1 tart apple, peeled and diced

2 small dilled pickles, diced
½ cup sour cream
2 tbls. cider vinegar
2 tsps. prepared mustard
salt and pepper to taste.

Combine herring, potatoes, beets, carrots, apple, and pickles in a medium bowl. Mix remaining ingredients and add to herring-vegetable mixture. Refrigerate 2 hours to blend flavors. Garnish with hard-cooked egg slices or tomato wedges.

BAKED HADDOCK

2 lbs. haddock fillets
½ tsp. salt
¼ tsp. pepper
dash of garlic powder
  and tarragon (optional)

⅓ cup sherry
1 cup cream of mushroom soup
½ cup buttered bread crumbs
½ cup grated Cheddar cheese

Cut haddock into serving pieces and place in buttered casserole. Sprinkle with seasonings. Add sherry to soup. Pour over fish in casserole, adding a small amount of water if necessary. Top with buttered crumbs; sprinkle with grated cheese. Bake at 350° for 25 to 30 minutes. Serves 4 to 6.

FINNAN HADDIE CASSEROLE

3 lbs. Finnan Haddie, skinned
   and boned
milk to cover
2 tbls. butter
1 small green pepper, diced
1 medium onion, diced

4 tbls. flour
1/8 tsp. salt
2½ cups warm milk
Paprika
buttered crumbs

Cut fish in 3 or 4 pieces; place in saucepan; cover with milk. Cook over low heat until fish flakes — about ½ hour. Melt butter in a large saucepan, add green pepper and onion; cook gently about 10 minutes. Add flour, stirring until smooth. Add salt and warm milk; cook, stirring constantly, until thick. Place drained fish into a greased casserole; pour sauce over fish. Sprinkle with crumbs and paprika. Bake at 400° for 10 minutes or until sauce bubbles. Serves 4 to 6.

BARBECUED FILLETS

2 lbs. fish fillets*
2 cups chopped onion
2 tbls. chopped green pepper
1 clove garlic, chopped
2 tbls. oil
1 can tomato sauce

2 tbls. lemon juice
1 tbls. Worcestershire
1 tbls. sugar
2 tsps. salt
¼ tsp. pepper

Cook onion, green pepper, and garlic in oil until tender. Add remaining ingredients; simmer, stirring occasionally, for 5 minutes. Cool. Cut fish into 6 portions; place in single layer in shallow dish. Pour sauce over fish and let stand at least 30 minutes, turning once. Remove fish; reserve sauce for basting. Place fish in well-greased, hinged, wire grills. Cook about 4 inches above moderately hot coals for 5 to 8 minutes. Baste; turn. Cook 5 to 8 minutes longer or until fish flakes easily. Serves 6.
*A firm fish such as salmon, trout, or halibut is recommended.

FLOUNDER FILLETS

1 cup fine cheese cracker crumbs
1 egg, beaten
6 flounder fillets

salt and pepper to taste
lemon juice

Dip fillets in egg which has been seasoned with salt and pepper, then dip in cheese cracker crumbs. Roll up and secure with toothpicks. Place in buttered shallow baking dish. Sprinkle with a few drops of lemon juice. Bake at 400° for 15 to 20 minutes. May be served with a cheese sauce. Serves 3 to 6.

FILLETS WITH ORANGE SAUCE

12 fillets
4 tbls. butter
2 tbls. flour
grated rind of 1 orange

1 cup orange juice
½ tsp. salt
1 tsp. white pepper

Arrange fillets in lightly buttered baking dish. In a saucepan, melt butter. Stir in flour; add orange juice, rind, and seasonings. Cook, stirring, until sauce thickens. Pour evenly over fillets. Bake uncovered at 400° for 20 minutes or until fish flakes easily. If desired, ½ clove of garlic, crushed, may be added to sauce. Serves 6.

OVEN FRIED FILLETS

1 lb. flounder fillets
3 tbls. milk
salt, pepper, and paprika

½ cup bread crumbs
3 tbls. butter, melted

Combine crumbs, seasonings to taste, and 2 tbls. melted butter. Pat fish dry on paper towels. Dip in milk, then in crumb mixture. Place fillets in greased, shallow baking dish; sprinkle with remaining tablespoon of melted butter. Bake in 450° oven for 15 minutes or until fish flakes easily.

TIMBALES OF SOLE WITH SHRIMP MOUSSE

1 lb. fillet of sole or flounder
2 tbls. lemon juice
lemon-pepper seasoning
½ lb. raw shrimp, shelled
   and deveined
2 egg whites

1 cup heavy cream
1 tsp. salt
1 tbls. ketchup
1 tbls. parsley
2 tbls. dry sherry
8 tsps. butter

Dry fish on paper towels. If fillets are large, split in half, lengthwise, so that there are enough separate pieces for 8 small molds. Brush each piece with lemon juice and sprinkle with lemon-pepper. Grease 8 timbale molds, small custard cups, or souffle molds. Line sides with fillets, dark side up. (Extra odd pieces can be used to line bottoms. Since each timbale will be coated with sauce, it is not necessary to be particularly fussy about lining the molds.) Put shrimp and all remaining ingredients into food processor and blend with metal blade till the consistency of whipped cream. Spoon into fish-lined molds. Put about 1 tsp. butter on top of mousse in each mold. Top with circles of waxed paper. (If food processor is not available, grind shrimp on fine blade of meat grinder and combine with remaining ingredients in blender or mixer at high speed.) Place timbales in large pan and add 1″ of boiling water to pan. Bake at 375° for 30 minutes or till mousse rises slightly and becomes just firm. Fish fillets should flake with a fork.

Sauce

¼ **cup butter**
¼ **cup flour**
½ **tsp. salt**
1 (10-oz.) pkg. fresh mushrooms, chopped & sautéed, but not drained

1 tbls. ketchup
2 egg yolks, slightly beaten
⅓ **cup dry sherry**
1 cup light cream

Melt butter. Add flour and salt and stir with whisk for 2 minutes. Add cream and ketchup, cooking till thickened. Stir a little sauce into egg yolks to warm the mixture, then stir back into cream mixture. Add sherry and stir over low heat till hot. Add mushrooms and their liquid. Remove timbales from molds, pouring accumulated liquid into sauce. Arrange on serving platter and cap with half the sauce. Pass remaining sauce. Serves 6 to 8.

CLAMS SOUTHSIDE

2 cups chopped clams
2 cups chopped celery
2 tbls. chopped onion
2 tbls. chopped parsley

1 pt. cream
2 tbls. butter
1 tbls. sherry
thin slices of toast, buttered

Melt butter in a skillet; add celery; cook until it begins to soften. Add onions and clams; add parsley when onions are almost limp. Do not let mixture brown. Brew on low heat about ¾ hour. Add cream; do **not** let cream come to a boil. When hot, add sherry. Spoon mixture onto toast. Serves 6.

CRAB AND ARTICHOKE CASSEROLE

1 lb. fresh crabmeat
1 pkg. frozen artichoke hearts, defrosted
1 can (3-oz.) sliced mushrooms, drained
1 pkg. (3-oz.) slivered almonds
¼ **cup minced onion**

½ **cup buttered crumbs**
2 tbls. flour
2 tbls. butter
1½ cups milk or light cream
¼ **cup dry Vermouth**
½ **cup grated Swiss cheese**

Sauté onions in a little butter or oil until softened; push to one side of pan; add almonds and saute until golden, adding oil if necessary. Cut artichokes in half; add to large bowl containing crabmeat; add mushrooms and onions. Make a cream sauce with butter, flour, milk, and Vermouth. Add mushroom juice. Bring to a light boil; stir in cheese; simmer, stirring, until cheese is melted and combined. Put crab mixture in shallow casserole; pour sauce over the mixture; sprinkle with buttered crumbs. Bake at 350° until bubbly (15-20 minutes).

CRAB AND SPINACH CASSEROLE

2 pkgs. frozen chopped spinach
   thawed, squeezed to remove as
   much moisture as possible
½ lb. grated sharp Cheddar
1 lb. crabmeat

1 tbls. minced onion
   (fresh or dried)
1 tbls. lemon juice
dash of nutmeg
butter

Sauce

1 tbls. butter
2 tbls. flour

1 can cream of tomato soup
1 cup sour cream

Place well drained spinach in bottom of flat, rectangular casserole. Sprinkle with one-half the grated cheddar. Mix crab, onion, lemon juice, and nutmeg; spread over cheese and spinach. Sprinkle with remaining cheese. Sauce: melt butter and blend in flour; add tomato soup and sour cream. Pour sauce over crab/spinach mixture. Dot with butter. Bake uncovered 30 minutes at 350° or 45 minutes at 325°. Serves 6.

CRABMEAT SALAD

1½ lbs. fresh crabmeat
1 cup sliced celery
2 tbls. minced onion
2 stalks scallion, sliced

½ cup shredded iceberg lettuce
½ cup mayonnaise
juice of ½ fresh lemon
¼ tsp. salt if desired

Break up crabmeat into 1″ pieces in large mixing bowl. Combine crabmeat with remaining ingredients. Toss lightly. Cover bowl and refrigerate for 2 hours. Remove from refrigerator and mix thoroughly. Serve on a bed of lettuce. Serves 6.

SUNDAY SUPPER

The Captain's choice, a great tureen of seafood chowder, to be ladled into matching pottery dishes made by the Davenport Factory in England c. 1850. On the mantel, a souvenir from the East — lead figures made in China c. 1870 representing Chinese perception of English servants.

Sunday Night Supper

Fish Chowder

Cheese Biscuits

Spinach Salad

Hot Salad Dressing

Lemon Mousse

Cookies

CELESTIAL OYSTERS

½ cup butter or margarine
½ cup chopped onion
⅓ cup chopped green pepper
1 clove garlic, minced
½ cup flour
1½ tsps. paprika
½ tsp. salt
¼ tsp. freshly ground pepper

1 tsp. Tabasco
dash cayenne
1 tbls. fresh lemon juice
1 tbls. Angostura bitters
1 tsp. finely grated lemon rind
2 cups oyster liquor
3 cups well-drained oysters
½ cup crushed saltines

Sauté onion, green pepper, and garlic in melted butter until onion is golden; stir in flour; cook over medium heat, stirring, until flour becomes golden. Add paprika, salt, pepper, cayenne, Tabasco, lemon juice, lemon rind, bitters, and oyster liquor. Stir over low heat until sauce bubbles and thickens. Stir in oysters. Pour mixture into greased 1½-quart shallow pan. Sprinkle top with cracker crumbs. Bake uncovered in 400° oven for 20-25 minutes, or until bubbly. Can also be served in individual ramekins; bake only 15-20 minutes. Serves 6-8.

OYSTER PIE

1 qt. oysters
light cream
1 tbls. butter
2 tbls. finely chopped celery
2 tbls. chopped parsley
3 hard-cooked egg yolks

½ cup bread crumbs
3 tbls. Sherry
1 tbls. grated onion
¼ lb. sliced fresh mushrooms
salt and pepper to taste
pastry for 9″ crust

Drain oysters well; add enough cream to liquor to make 1½ cups; add celery, parsley, and butter; bring to a boil. Remove from heat. Mash egg yolks with crumbs and sherry; stir into hot mixture slowly. Return to heat; cook until thickened and smooth. Season with onion, salt and pepper. Spread oysters in lightly buttered 9-inch pie plate; cover with mushrooms; pour sauce over all. Cover with pastry. Brush with milk. Bake at 375° for 30 minutes until pastry is browned. Serves 4 to 6.

OYSTERS TERRAPIN

1 pt. oysters, cut in halves	1 recipe white sauce
1 lb. mushrooms, sliced	Toast or toast cups
3 onions, sliced	butter

Cook onions in a little butter until light brown; add mushrooms and continue cooking for 15 minutes. Drain off any remaining liquid. Add the cut-up oysters. Add white sauce and cook gently for 5 to 7 minutes. Serve on toast. Serves 2 to 4.

SCALLOPED OYSTERS

1 pint oysters (drained)	1 cup cracker crumbs
4 tbls. oyster liquid	½ cup dry bread crumbs
½ cup melted butter	salt & pepper to taste
2 tbls. cream or milk	

Mix bread and cracker crumbs; stir in melted butter. Put a layer of crumb mixture in bottom of flat casserole (greased); cover with oysters; sprinkle with salt and pepper. Repeat both layers. Top with crumb layer. Bake at 450° for 30 minutes. (Never more than 2 layers.) For cracker crumbs, substitute ½ cup crushed potato chips and ½ cup cracker crumbs. Do not use salt if crackers and/or chips are salted. Serves 2 generously as main course.

BAKED "BLUE EYED" SCALLOPS

1 pint Cape scallops (blue-eyed)	¼ cup melted butter
½ cup soft bread crumbs	nutmeg
½ cup finely crumbled potato chips	⅓ cup light cream

Mix crumbs with melted butter; sprinkle half the crumbs over the bottom of a shallow baking dish. Carefully place scallops on top of crumbs, as close together as possible without overlapping. Sprinkle very lightly with nutmeg. Sprinkle rest of crumbs over top. Just before baking, pour cream carefully around sides of casserole, taking care not to pour it directly over the scallops. Bake in 350° oven about 35 minutes. Serves 2 to 4. Recipe may be doubled: layer a second pint of scallops over the crumbs covering the first; sprinkle with additional nutmeg and ½ cup mixed crumbs. Use ½ cup cream. **Never** have more than 2 layers of scallops.

SHRIMP MADELEINE

3 tbls. dry English mustard
4 tbls. butter
3 lbs. shrimp

⅓ cup brandy
2 cups heavy cream
salt and pepper

Mix mustard with just enough water to make a light paste. Melt butter over high heat and sauté the shrimp a few minutes — just long enough for all water to evaporate from them. Warm the brandy; pour it over the shrimp and ignite. When the flames subside, add cream slowly, stirring, until a smooth sauce is obtained. Add mustard and salt and pepper to taste. Serve in individual casserole dishes or on a platter. Garnish with parsley.

ARTICHOKE AND SHRIMP CASSEROLE

1 pkg. frozen artichoke hearts
defrosted
1 lb. fresh cooked shrimp, shelled
and cleaned
¼ lb. mushrooms, sliced
2 tbls. flour
2 tbls. butter

1½ cups light cream or milk
¼ cup dry sherry
1 tbls. Worcestershire
¼ cup soft bread crumbs
2 tbls. Parmesan cheese
salt and pepper to taste
paprika

Let artichokes defrost in very little boiling water just until they can be separated. Spread over bottom of a buttered baking dish. Spread cooked shrimp over the artichokes. Sauté sliced mushrooms in a little butter or cooking oil 4 to 5 minutes. Spread over artichokes and shrimp. Make a cream sauce with butter, flour, and light cream; salt and pepper to taste; add sherry and Worcestershire; pour over shrimp mixture. Mix crumbs with paprika and cheese; sprinkle over top. Bake about 20 minutes at 375°. Sprinkle with a little chopped parsley before serving. Serves 4 to 6. White meat of chicken may be substituted for shrimp.

SWEET AND SOUR SHRIMP

2 lbs. shrimp, shelled and cleaned
3 tbls. butter or margarine, melted
2½ cups pineapple chunks with juice
2 tbls. slivered candied ginger
1 green pepper, cut in strips

½ cup vinegar
½ cup sugar
pinch of salt
1 tbls. soy sauce
2½ tbls. cornstarch

Toss shrimp in melted butter; cook about 5 minutes, stirring occasionally. Add pineapple chunks and juice, green pepper strips, ginger, vinegar, sugar, salt, and soy sauce. Cook over low heat about 2 minutes. Spoon 2 tablespoons of this mixture into the cornstarch; mix to a smooth paste. Return to shrimp mixture; cook slowly, stirring, until liquid is thickened slightly and transparent. Serve over rice. Serves 6.

SHRIMP AND EGG CASSEROLE

8 eggs, hard boiled
½ tsp. salt
½ tsp. sharp mustard
¼ cup mayonnaise
2 lbs. cooked shrimp

2 3-oz. cans sliced mushrooms, drained
1 tbls. onion flakes
4 cups cream sauce
½ cup grated Swiss cheese

Halve the eggs; remove yolks and mash with mayonnaise, salt, and mustard. Fill whites with yolk mixture; cut halves into quarters lengthwise. Place eggs in three rows in a greased 9″ x 12″ baking dish. Spread shrimp over eggs; scatter mushrooms and onion flakes over shrimp and eggs. Dish may now be covered with plastic wrap and refrigerated several hours. Mix cream sauce with grated Swiss (mild Cheddar may be substituted). Heat, stirring, until cheese is melted and combined; pour over shrimp mixture. Bake immediately in a 400° oven until bubbly (about 20 minutes). Do not freeze. Serves 6 to 8.

BAKED STUFFED SHRIMP

6-8 jumbo shrimp
1 stack saltines or butter crackers
½ cup vegetable oil
½ cup Parmesan cheese

½ stick butter
1 tsp. parsley
¼ tsp. garlic powder

Shell raw shrimp, being careful to retain tail. Split down center of back almost through and spread open in shallow baking dish. Crumble crackers finely. Mix with other ingredients. Pile on shrimp. May be prepared ahead. Bake at 350° for 15-20 minutes. Serves 2 to 3. May be doubled.

SHRIMP-CHEESE CASSEROLE

6 slices day-old bread
1 lb. shrimp cooked, peeled &
    deveined
½ lb. Cheddar cheese, diced
3 eggs (beaten)

4 tbls. butter, melted
¼ tsp. dry mustard
¼ tsp. basil
salt, pepper to taste
1 cup milk

Trim bread and cut in cubes. Arrange layers of bread, shrimp, and cheese and pour melted butter over all. Beat eggs and add mustard, basil, salt, and pepper. Stir in milk and pour this mixture over the layers of shrimp, bread and cheese. Refrigerate over night, if desired. Bake at 350° one hour, covered. Serve hot. Serves 4-6.

SUMMERTIME LUNCHEON MOUSSE

1 8-oz. pkg. cream cheese
1 can tomato soup
2 tbls. gelatin
½ cup cold water
½ cup celery, chopped

¼ cup green pepper, chopped
¼ cup onion, chopped
1 cup mayonnaise
1½ cans (10-oz.) shrimp, crab, or
    tuna

Soften gelatin in cold water. Heat tomato soup; add cheese; stir until cheese has melted. Remove from heat; add gelatin. Refrigerate until mixture begins to gel. Stir in remaining ingredients. Spoon into 7½" by 11" glass dish; refrigerate several hours or overnight. Cut in squares; serve on lettuce. Serves 10 to 12. One half the recipe fills 5 custard cups.

LOBSTER MOUSSE

3 envelopes plain gelatin
½ cup water
3 cups boiling water
4 cubes chicken bouillon
1 cup mayonnaise
½ cup celery, chopped fine
¼ cup drained capers

2 dashes hot pepper sauce
4 tbls. lemon juice
2 tbls. grated onion
1 tsp. paprika
¾ cup heavy cream, whipped
4 cups lobster meat, chopped
    (shrimp may be substituted)

Soften gelatin in ½ cup water; dissolve in boiling water to which bouillon cubes have been added. Cool. Add mayonnaise, pepper sauce, lemon juice, onion, and paprika. Chill until it begins to thicken. Fold in lobster meat, whipped cream, celery, and capers. Pour into 6-cup mold, refrigerate until set. Serves 10 to 12.

LOBSTER-RICE SOUFFLÉ

¼ cup raw rice
¼ tsp. salt
¾ cup boiling water
4 eggs, separated
4 tbls. butter or margarine
4 tbls. flour
½ tsp. salt
1 cup milk
1 can (6-oz.) lobster meat, drained,
  boned, cut into bite-size pieces

Cheese Sauce
2 tbls. butter
2 tbls. flour
½ tsp. dry mustard
½ tsp. salt
1½ cups milk
1 cup grated cheese or pieces of
  processed cheese

Stir rice and salt into boiling water, cover and simmer 20 minutes or until water is absorbed. Separate eggs, putting whites into medium size bowl; yolks into large bowl. Melt butter or margarine. Stir in flour and ½ tsp. salt; cook, stirring all the time, until mixture bubbles. Stir in milk slowly; continue cooking and stirring until sauce is very thick and boils 1 minute; remove from heat. Beat egg yolks well; slowly stir in cream sauce, cooked rice, and lobster. Lightly fold in stiffly beaten egg whites until no streaks of sauce or egg white remain. Pour into ungreased, 8-cup, deep baking dish. Set dish in baking pan on oven shelf; pour in boiling water to depth of 1 inch. Bake in slow oven (325°) 1 hour, or until top is firm and puffy golden. Serve at once with cheese sauce.
Cheese Sauce: melt butter, add flour, salt, mustard. Stir until mixture bubbles. Stir in milk slowly. Continue cooking and stirring until sauce thickens and boils 1 minute. Stir in cheese until melted and combined.

LOBSTER THERMIDOR

2 live lobsters (1½ lbs. each)
1½ cups water
1 small onion, sliced
1 small carrot, sliced
1 bay leaf

Sauce
1 large onion, thinly sliced
1 tbls. butter
½ cup dry white wine
2 cups thick white sauce
½ tsp. dry mustard
4 tbls. grated Parmesan
dash of salt, pepper, and paprika

Make a stock of water, onion, carrot, and bay leaf; bring to a boil. Add lobsters; bring to a boil again. Remove lobsters; turn onto backs. With a sharp knife, slit lobsters down middle seam from behind eyes to end of tail. Remove the sac behind the eyes and the vein which extends to end of tail. Cut off claws; remove meat. Remove tail meat. Cut all meat into bite-size pieces. Remove coral, if any, and green tomalley. Cook second onion quickly in 1 tbls. of butter. Add white wine; bring to boil and cook until liquid evaporates. Mix into cream sauce; add mustard, Parmesan, paprika, coral, and tomalley. Sauce should be consistency of heavy cream. With kitchen shears, cut lobster shells in half lengthwise; place on a flat baking dish. Mix lobster meat with sauce, fill shells. Sprinkle with grated cheese. Place under broiler until tops begin to brown, 20 to 30 minutes. Serves 4.

BAKED STUFFED LOBSTER

1 (or more) 1½ lb. lobster, split, intestinal vein and stomach removed.

Dressing (per lobster):

4 to 5 common crackers, finely crushed	**tomalley (green liver) from lobster**
1 slice white bread, crumbled	**melted butter**
	salt and pepper

In large bowl, mix cracker crumbs, crumbled bread, and tomalley. Use fingers to do this so that tomalley will be finely distributed. Add enough melted butter to make dressing very moist. Salt and pepper to taste. (Variations: add a tablespoon of minced onion or Parmesan cheese.) Fill body cavity with dressing, extending some into split section of tail. Extra dressing may be mounded over body section or baked in a separate pan. If a very moist dressing is desired, more melted butter may be poured over the dressing at this time. Bake in roasting pan at 350° for 25 minutes. Serves 1. To split a live lobster: turn lobster on back; cross large claws; cover claws with folded towel. Holding lobster with both hands, slap sharply on counter to stun. With sharp-pointed butcher knife, make a deep incision just behind eyes and draw knife quickly down the middle of the body and entire length of tail, being careful not to cut through the lobster's back shell. Hold lobster firmly while doing this. Spread the lobster open; remove stomach sac behind eyes and intestinal vein which extends to end of tail. Remove green liver (tomalley) and add to dressing, or mash it and serve on saltines as a spread. The red coral, found in females, is also edible and considered a delicacy by many.

LOBSTER NEWBURG

2 lbs. cooked lobster meat	**4 egg yolks**
½ lb. butter	**1 pt. light cream**
5 tbls. sherry	**4 to 6 slices toast**

Cut lobster into bite-size pieces; sauté in butter and sherry until thoroughly heated. Do not overcook as lobster will toughen. Stir while heating. Mix together lightly the egg yolks and cream; add to lobster and stir slowly until sauce begins to thicken. Serve on toast triangles. Serves 4 to 6.

REGATTA ROUX

2 lbs. fish fillets (cod, haddock,
   sole, hake)
1 cup mayonnaise
1 10-oz. can mushroom soup
1 cup sour cream
salt and pepper to taste

½ cup Chablis
1 6-oz. can crabmeat, drained, liquid
   reserved
1 tbls. dry onion flakes
½ tsp. thyme or 2 sprigs

Put mayonnaise, soup, sour cream, and Chablis in a 4-qt. saucepan. Whisk to blend; add onion, thyme, and crabmeat. Bring to simmer; do **not** boil. Remove from heat; keep warm. Place fish in greased baking dish; pour reserved crab liquid over fish; add just enough water to cover bottom of dish. Cover with foil; bake at 400° for 10 minutes. Remove foil; broil for 5 minutes. Drain. Add fish to warm sauce very gently. Serve with rice. Serves 4. Instead of adding fish to sauce, fish may be placed in a heated serving dish with sauce poured over the fish.

GOURMET SEAFOOD SCALLOP

1 8-oz. pkg. frozen shrimp or
   2 4-oz. cans of shrimp
1 12-oz. pkg. frozen scallops
1 7-oz. can crabmeat
1 4-oz. can sliced mushrooms
5 tbls. margarine
¼ cup flour

1½ cups milk, approximately
1 tsp. salt
¾ tsp. Worcestershire
1 drop Tabasco
1 cup shredded sharp Cheddar
¼ cup bread crumbs

Cook frozen shrimp and scallops according to package directions. Drain mushrooms, reserving liquid. In large casserole, combine shrimp, scallops, crab, and mushrooms; toss lightly with fork to mix. **Sauce:** melt 4 tbls. margarine in saucepan; add flour, stirring until smooth. Add enough milk to mushroom liquor to make 2 cups; stir into roux; continue stirring until thickened. Add salt, Worcestershire, Tabasco, and ½ cup cheese. Stir until cheese is melted and combined. Pour over seafood. Melt remaining tablespoon butter; mix with bread crumbs and remaining cheese. Sprinkle over mixture. Bake at 375° for 25 minutes. Serves 8.

SEAFOOD LASAGNA

8 lasagna noodles
1 cup chopped onion
2 tbls. butter or margarine
1 8-oz. pkg. cream cheese (softened)
1½ cups cream style cottage cheese
1 beaten egg
½ lb. fresh mushrooms
2 tsps. dried basil, crushed
2 cans condensed cream of
   mushroom soup

⅓ cup milk
⅓ cup dry white wine
1 lb. shelled shrimp (cooked and
   halved)
1 7½-oz. can crab, drained, flaked
   and cartilage removed
¼ cup grated parmesan cheese
½ cup (2 ozs.) shredded sharp
   American cheese

Cook lasagna noodles according to package directions; drain. Arrange 4 noodles in bottom of greased 13 x 9 x 2-inch baking dish. Cook onion and mushrooms in butter or margarine till tender; blend in cream cheese. Stir in cottage cheese, egg, basil, ½ teaspoon salt, and 1/8 teaspoon pepper; spread half atop noodles. Combine soup, milk, and wine. Stir in shrimp and crab; spread half over cottage cheese layer. Repeat layers. Sprinkle with parmesan. Bake uncovered in 350 degrees oven for 45 minutes. Top with American cheese. Bake 2 to 3 minutes more. Let stand 15 minutes before serving. Makes 12 servings.

CIOPPINO

1 cup olive or cooking oil
3 cloves garlic, minced
1½ cups chopped onion
¾ cup chopped green pepper
¾ cup chopped green onion
1 can baby clams
1 can Italian plum tomatoes
   (2 lbs. 3 ozs.)
1 can tomato paste (6 ozs.)
1 cup chopped parsley

2 tbls. oregano
½ tsp. basil
2 tsps. salt
¼ tsp. pepper
1¾ cups Burgundy
¾ cup water
1 can crabmeat (½ lb. fresh)
¼ lb. raw shrimp, shelled
1 lb. halibut, haddock, or
   cusk

In a 6-qt. kettle, sauté the garlic, onions, and green pepper in oil until tender, about 10 minutes. Drain clams; reserve ¼ cup of liquid. Add to clam liquid the undrained tomatoes, tomato paste, Burgundy, parsley, oregano, basil, salt, pepper, and ¾ cup water. Add to garlic mixture; mix well. Bring to a boil; reduce heat; simmer, uncovered, stirring for 10 minutes. Remove any skin from fish; cut into 1-inch cubes. Add to mixture; add shrimp and crab. Simmer uncovered for 15 minutes. Serves 6. If made ahead, do not add crab until warming up.

BREAST OF CHICKEN SAM WARD

6 large boned chicken breasts
flour
2 eggs
6 tbls. butter
bread crumbs
6 slices of bacon, cooked

8 mushrooms, sliced
2 shallots, chopped
2 tbls. sherry
3 cups light cream sauce
salt and pepper to taste

Season chicken breasts with salt and pepper; then bread them, dipping first in flour, then beaten eggs, and finally finely sieved bread crumbs. Heat 4 tablespoons butter in sauté pan and cook chicken about 15 minutes on each side or until done. Sauté the mushrooms with the shallots in 2 tablespoons of butter; add the sherry wine; simmer a few minutes. Add cream sauce, season, and serve by putting the mushroom sauce on a plate, then the chicken breast, and finally the bacon. Serves 6.

BREAST OF CHICKEN NORMANDY

4 to 6 whole chicken breasts,
   boned and flattened
salt and pepper to taste
½ tsp. powdered thyme
2 tbls. finely chopped onion
1 4-oz. can chopped mushrooms
   drained

½ cup butter
½ lb. chicken livers, chopped
½ cup Swiss cheese, grated
1 egg, beaten
fine bread crumbs

Sprinkle flattened chicken inside with salt, pepper, and thyme. Heat ¼ cup of the butter; add livers and onion; sprinkle with salt. Cook slowly for about 5 minutes until livers are done. Remove from heat; stir in mushrooms and cheese. Divide into 4 to 6 portions; place in center of breasts. Fold sides over stuffing and secure with wooden picks. Roll in beaten egg and then in crumbs. Refrigerate uncovered at least 2 hours to allow coating to dry. Heat remaining ¼ cup butter in a large skillet; add breasts, and brown on both sides. Remove to shallow pan; bake at 350° for 45 minutes. Serve with supreme sauce. Serves 4 to 6.

SUPREME SAUCE

¼ cup butter
¼ cup flour
2 cups chicken stock or
   canned bouillon

1 tbls. lemon juice
½ cup light cream

Melt butter; blend in flour. Add chicken stock slowly. Cook, stirring constantly, until mixture thickens and boils. Boil gently 3 to 5 minutes, stirring. Add lemon juice. Stir in cream slowly. Heat but do **not** boil. Makes approximately 3 cups.

HONEY-LEMON CHICKEN

1 - 3 to 3½ lb. frying chicken
  cut up
½ cup honey
1 cup ketchup

1 large lemon sliced thin
1 1-lb. 13-oz. can peach halves
salt and pepper to taste

Arrange chicken pieces in a shallow baking dish. Season with salt and pepper. Combine ketchup and honey and pour over chicken, turning to coat all sides. Place lemon slices over chicken pieces. Bake uncovered 1 hour or until tender at 325°, turning once while baking. During the last 15 minutes increase heat to 350°. Arrange well drained peach halves around chicken pieces. Baste with sauce. Serves 4.

CHICKEN AND ENDIVE PARMESAN

3 whole chicken breasts, skinned
  and boned
3 peppercorns
3 stalks celery
1 small onion, sliced
6 heads Belgian endive
1¼ cups chicken broth
2 tbls. capers

¼ tbls. celery seed
1 tbls. butter
1 tbls. flour
2 cups light cream
salt and pepper to taste
1 cup grated Parmesan cheese
½ cup butter bread crumbs
2 tbls. parsley, chopped

Steam chicken breasts in lightly salted water to cover to which has been added the peppercorns, celery, and onions. When chicken is tender, strain; reserve 1¼ cups broth. Cut chicken into large strips and place on bottom of shallow, lightly greased, casserole. Cut endives in half the long way. Cut out center bitter heart at stem end, leaving enough heart to hold the half together. Place in skillet; cover with reserved broth; steam gently about 30 minutes, turning carefully once or twice. Remove endive from broth; place on top of chicken; sprinkle with capers and celery seed.

Make a cheese sauce with butter, flour, salt and pepper to taste, and light cream. Stir over low heat until thickened. Add cheese. If too thick, thin with one or two tablespoons chicken stock. Pour over chicken, sprinkle with buttered crumbs and parsley. Bake at 350° for 30 minutes. Serves 6 to 8.

LIVELY, COLORFUL, GOOD TASTING CHICKEN

2-3 lbs. cut-up chicken	any or all of the following sliced:
½ lb. bacon	potatoes mushrooms
salt and pepper	celery onions
bay leaf	turnips green peppers
rosemary	carrots tomatoes

Line casserole with bacon strips. Put chicken pieces on top of bacon; sprinkle salt and pepper on chicken. Add sliced vegetables on top. Sprinkle bay leaf and rosemary on vegetables. Cover with foil and bake at 375° for 1 to 1½ hours. Baste a couple of times with juice from bottom of casserole. Serves 6-8.

GRANDMOTHER'S LUNCHEON CASSEROLE: CHICKEN WITH MUSTARD AND APPLES

2 cups diced white meat of chicken	⅓ cup light cream
1 tbls. prepared brown mustard	½ cup soft bread crumbs
1 tbls. lemon juice	1 can sliced apples
½ tsp. salt	4 tbls. melted butter
1 can cream of mushroom soup	

Combine the chicken and mustard and spread in a buttered baking dish; top with apple slices. Sprinkle with salt and lemon juice. Combine soup and cream; pour over all. Top with crumbs which have been tossed in melted butter. Completely cover with the crumbs. Bake in 350° oven uncovered for 30 minutes. Serves 4.

BARBIE'S CHICKEN DIVAN

3 chicken breasts (whole), cooked and boned	½ tsp. curry powder (scant)
2 pkgs. frozen broccoli	2 tbls. sherry
2 cans cream of chicken soup	1 cup sharp cheese shredded or Parmesan cheese
1 cup mayonnaise	1 cup buttered bread crumbs
1 tsp. lemon juice	

Defrost brocolli and drain. Combine soup, mayonnaise, lemon juice, curry powder, and sherry. Pour over chicken and brocolli which has been layered in a casserole dish. Spread the cheese and then the bread crumbs over the casserole. Bake at 350° 1 hour. Serves 6 to 8.

BUKHARI CHICKEN (SAUDI ARABIA)

4 chicken breasts, split and boned
1 tsp. salt
1½ cups chicken bouillon
¼ cup butter, melted
1 tbls. soy sauce
1 or more tsp. ground ginger

1 cup celery, diced
1 onion, sliced
1 green pepper cut in strips
1 4-oz. can mushrooms (sliced)
1 cup water
2 tbls. cornstarch
1 cup or more shredded cabbage

Sprinkle chicken with salt. Brown in melted butter. Add bouillon, soy sauce, ginger, and celery. Cover. Simmer 25 minutes. Add onion, green pepper, and musorooms with liquid. Cover; simmer 10 minutes. Add blended cornstarch and water. Cook, stirring, until thickened. Add cabbage; cover. Cook 3 minutes. Serves 4.

CHICKEN AND CUCUMBER CASSEROLE

1 3-lb. chicken, cut in pieces
1 onion, chopped
2 stalks celery, chopped
1 carrot, peeled and chopped
½ tsp. thyme

2 sprigs parsley
2 cups chicken broth or 1½ cups
    broth and ½ cup Vermouth
½ tsp. dill weed
salt and pepper to taste

Sauce

2 tbls. cornstarch dissolved in water
¼ tsp. dill weed
½ cup sour cream or yogurt
salt and pepper to taste

1 small cucumber
2 tbls. butter
2 tbls. finely chopped parsley

Place chicken in casserole. Place remaining ingredients over chicken; cover and cook at 350° 1 hour. Keep chicken warm; strain and boil down broth until 1 cup remains. Stir cornstarch into cold water, thvn add to broth; season with salt and pepper and dill weed; stir in sour cream or yogurt. Peel cucumber and seed; cut into 1″ pieces; sauté in butter until soft but still crunchy. Pour the sauce over the chicken; add the cucumbers and parsley. Serves 4.

CHICKEN CORDON GOLD

12 chicken breasts, pounded thin
2 pkgs. Boursin herbed cheese
12 slices Prosciutto or deli ham
¾ cup butter melted
1 cup chicken stock

¾ cup Galliano Liqueur
½ lb. sliced fresh mushrooms
1 bunch coarsely chopped parsley
1 cup flour
salt and pepper

Dredge each chicken breast in a little flour mixed with pepper and salt. Layer each breast with a couple of tablespoons of Boursin, then a slice of ham. Roll up each breast, secure it with toothpicks, and close up the ends with toothpicks. Brown each rolled breast lightly in a quarter cup of melted butter. Pour in a cup of chicken broth and half a cup of Galliano. Cover the skillet and simmer slowly until breasts are tender, about 30 minutes. In another skillet, heat a half cup of butter and two tablespoons of Galliano. Add the mushrooms and sauté 5 to 8 minutes. Add the parsley and sauté another 3 minutes. Add this sauce to the chicken five minutes before it is done. Remove toothpicks before serving. Serves 6-8. Serve over saffron rice or buttered noodles.

MOUNT FUJI CHICKEN

2 cups celery, cut on bias
1 large onion, sliced thin
1 can mushroom soup
¼ cup chicken stock
2-3 tsps. soy sauce

2 cups cooked chicken, cubed
1 can water chestnuts, sliced thin
1 can Chinese noodles
1 small pkg. sliced almonds

Sauté until transparent the celery and onions. Add the soup, chicken stock, soy sauce. Cook over low heat until well blended. This may be done ahead. Reheat and add the chicken and water chestnuts. Top with the Chinese noodles and almonds. Bake at 350° about 20 - 30 minutes.

CHICKEN JUBILEE

2 whole chicken breasts, split,
    skinned, and boned
1 small can Bing cherries
1 tbls. cornstarch

¼ cup cherry brandy or port wine
¼ cup currant jelly
1 cup sour cream
salt and pepper to taste

Steam chicken breasts until tender; place in bottom of a shallow, lightly greased casserole. Drain cherries; blend juice with cornstarch; add brandy and jelly; simmer until thickened, stirring. Add cherries and bring to a boil; remove from heat; stir in the sour cream; pour over chicken. Bake at 350° until bubbly — 20 to 30 minutes. Serves 4.

POULET AU CITRON

2 lbs. boneless chicken breasts
1 cup sour cream
¼ cup lemon juice
3 tsps. Worcestershire sauce
3 tsps. celery salt
1/8 tsp. pepper

20 unsalted cracked wheat
   wafers
2 tbls. melted butter
1 tbls. parsley
1/8 tsp. pepper

Place chicken in oven to table serving pan. Mix sour cream, lemon juice, Worcestershire sauce, celery salt, and pepper. Pour over chicken and marinate all day. Crunch up the cracked wheat crackers; add the butter, parsley, and pepper and sprinkle mixture over chicken before baking. Shake paprika on top. Bake at 350° 1 hour.

CHICKEN ROSÉ

3 chicken breasts, split, and skin
   removed (boned or unboned)
¼ cup Rosé wine
¼ cup soy sauce
¼ cup salad or olive oil

2 tbls. water
1 clove garlic, sliced
1 tsp. ground ginger
¼ tsp. oregano
1 tbls. brown sugar

Combine all ingredients except chicken; stir to mix well. Arrange chicken in one or two layers in baking dish. Pour wine mixture over chicken. Cover and bake about 1½ hours in 350° oven.

GINGER CHICKEN

3½ lbs. boned chicken
¾ cup chopped scallions
4 cloves crushed garlic
3 tbls. salad oil
¼ to ½ cup minced fresh or
   crystallized ginger

3 tbls. soy sauce
3 tbls. vinegar
1½ tbls. sugar
¼ tsp. salt and pepper
½ cup stock
1 cup sliced mushrooms

You can cook this in a wok or skillet. Cut chicken into small pieces but do not dice. Sauté scallions and garlic in oil. Add ginger, soy sauce, vinegar and sugar. Stir until sugar dissolves. Add chicken and stir fry 3 minutes. Add salt, pepper, and stock. Bring to boil; cover and simmer until chicken is done, about ½ hour. Add mushrooms and cook for additional 10 minutes. Serves 4. Serve with rice, plain or curried.

CHICKEN PARISIAN

4 chicken breasts, boned, skinned,
   and split
½ lb. sliced mushrooms
1 tbls. finely minced onion
1 can mushroom soup

1 cup sour cream
¼ to ⅓ cup sherry
paprika
lemon juice
1 tbls. butter
salt and pepper

Place chicken breasts in shallow casserole. Sprinkle with salt and pepper. Sauté onions and mushrooms in 1 tablespoon butter. When coated, add a little lemon juice; cook about 5 minutes. Add to chicken. Combine soup, sour cream, and sherry; pour over chicken and mushrooms. Sprinkle with paprika. Bake in 350° oven for 1 hour.

CHICKEN PUFF LOUISE

1 can cream of mushroom or celery
   soup
⅓ cup milk or Sauterne
1½ cups cooked chicken,
   cubed

1½ cups green beans, cooked and
   drained
4 eggs separated
¼ cup shredded Swiss or mild
   cheddar cheese

Combine soup and milk in 1½ quart casserole; stir in chicken and beans. Bake in 375° oven for 10 minutes. Beat egg yolks well; add cheese. Beat egg whites until stiff; fold into cheese-yolk mixture. Pile on top of hot chicken mixture; continue baking about ½ hour. If frozen beans are used cook only until separated before adding to chicken.

CHICKEN CHOP SUEY

1 lb. chicken, cooked
4 tbls. chicken fat or other oil
1 cup celery, cut in thin diagonal
   slices
1 onion, thinly sliced
6 large mushrooms, sliced
6 water chestnuts, sliced

½ lb. bean sprouts
¼ lb. bamboo shoots, cut diamond-
   shape
1 tbls. soy sauce
2 cups chicken stock
salt and pepper to taste

Cut cooked chicken into one-inch strips. Cook vegetables 5 minutes in half the fat; add chicken and remaining fat. Add bean sprouts, bamboo shoots, soy sauce, and stock. Simmer gently until well cooked (8-10 minutes). Add water chestnuts last 5 minutes. Season with salt and pepper. Serve on rice with chinese noodles. Crab, shrimp, or lobster may be substituted for chicken.

A TRADITIONAL HUNT BREAKFAST

A Sheraton style Salem sideboard displays the collection
of unusual serving pieces, glass and china that will be used for
the sumptuous meal prepared for the hungry fox hunters. The
centerpiece on the table is a complete hunt scene of carved
English figures and animals.

Traditional North Shore Hunt Breakfast

Orange Juice

Sausage Patties   *Fried Apple Slices*

Drunken Beans

Baked Virginia Ham

Cornbread

Honey, Butter, Marmalade

Blueberry Pie   *Apple Pie*

Coffee

Rum

CHICKEN "LASAGNE"

7-8 oz. lasagne noodles
1½ cups cream style cottage cheese*
3 cups diced cooked chicken
6-oz. grated sharp cheddar
¼ cup grated Parmesan
Mushroom Sauce:
½ cup chopped onion
½ cup green peppers, chopped

2 tbls. butter (margarine)
1 10¾-oz. can cream of chicken soup
¼ cup milk
1 6-oz. can chopped mushrooms, drained
¼ cup chopped pimiento
½ tsp. basil

Mushroom sauce: sauté onions and green peppers in butter; stir in chopped mushrooms, pimiento, basil, soup, and milk.

Cook noodles until tender following package directions. Drain and rinse in cold water. Butter a 9″ x 13″ x 2″ baking dish; layer half the noodles on bottom; cover with half the mushroom sauce; half the cottage cheese; half the chicken; half the cheddar cheese. Sprinkle with Parmesan cheese. Repeat all layers. Bake at 350° for 45 minutes. May be frozen. Serves 8 to 10.

*Low-cal cottage cheese may be used.

PARTY CHICKEN FOR 25

10 large chicken breasts, boned
3 pts. sour cream
5 cans cream of chicken soup
1¼ cups dry sherry or chablis
½ cup dehydrated onion flakes

5 4-oz. cans water chestnuts, drained and sliced
2½ cups sliced and pitted black olives
4 cups grated sharp Cheddar cheese

The day before serving: poach breasts in water to cover with a clove-studded onion, 6-8 whole peppercorns, 1 carrot, 1 bay leaf and a stalk of celery. Simmer gently until breasts are tender. Remove breasts and refrigerate. Day of party: mix sour cream, soup and wine together in large pot. Cut chicken into bite-size pieces and add to mixture. Add remaining ingredients and heat slowly until cheese melts and mixture is piping hot. Do not boil. Serve on a bed of Chinese noodles.

PARTY CHICKEN FOR 6

2½ chicken breasts
1½ cups sour cream
1 can cream of chicken soup
⅓ cup dry sherry

2 tbls. onion flakes
1 4-oz. can water chestnuts
¾ cup sliced black olives
1 cup sharp Cheddar cheese

Follow directions above.

CHICKEN BREASTS EN GELÉE

6 whole chicken breasts
2 cups water
1 small onion, sliced
2 celery tops
2 bay leaves
1 tsp. Accent
1 tsp. salt

¼ tsp. pepper
1 envelope plain gelatin
½ tsp. onion salt
1 cup dairy sour cream
½ tsp. tarragon
sliced raw carrots and radishes
scallion strips

Halve chicken breasts; bone; remove skin; place in large saucepan with water, onion, celery tops, bay leaves, Accent, salt, and pepper. Simmer, covered, 45 to 60 minutes (until tender). Remove from heat; strain broth; refrigerate chicken and broth separately at once. When cool, skim fat from chicken broth; measure ¾ cup broth into saucepan; add gelatin to soften; stir over low heat until the gelatin is dissolved. Add another ¾ cup of broth; stir in onion salt, sour cream, and tarragon. Chill until slightly thickened. Dip chicken breasts in gelatin mixture; place on wire rack over a cookie sheet. Chill; collect drippings; soften if necessary over low heat. Decorate tops with "flowers" of carrot and radish rings and scallion strips for stems. Spoon a layer of gelatin mixture over all. Chill until ready to serve and gelatin hardens. Serves 12.

CHICKEN SALAD SUPREME

2½ cups diced cold chicken
1 cup celery, chopped fine
1 cup sliced white grapes
½ cup shredded browned almonds

2 tbls. minced parsley
1 tsp. salt
1 cup mayonnaise
½ cup whipping cream, whipped

Combine and serve in lettuce cups. Serves 6.

CURRIED CHICKEN CRÊPES

Crêpes:
3 eggs
1 cup flour
1/8 tsp. salt
1 cup milk
¼ cup water
2 tbls. butter or margarine

Curried Chicken:
2 cups diced cooked chicken
¼ cup butter
1 cup diced celery
½ cup chopped onion
2 tbls. flour
1 tsp. salt
½ tsp. curry powder
chicken bouillon cube
1½ cups milk
½ cup raisins
Parmesan cheese

Crêpes: Beat 3 eggs well with fork. Add 1 cup flour and 1/8 tsp. salt, milk, and water. Continue beating until smooth. Melt 2 tbls. butter in a crepe or omelet pan. Heat until just hot, not smoking. For each crêpe, pour in 3 tbls. batter. Tilt pan from side to side to cover bottom. Cook about 1 minute or until solid. Quickly turn to other side for 30 seconds. Makes 12-14 crepes. **Curried Chicken:** Sauté celery and onion in melted butter until tender. Add flour and seasonings. Stir until well blended. Gradually add milk; add bouillon cube. Continue stirring until cube has dissolved and sauce has thickened. Fold in chicken and raisins; heat through. Place 2 heaping tablespoons filling in the center of each crêpe. Fold over both sides. Place crêpes in a baking dish. Smooth remaining sauce over crêpes. Sprinkle with Parmesan cheese. Bake at 375° for 15 minutes or until sauce bubbles. Will serve 6.

CORNISH GAME HEN CASSEROLE

2 Cornish game hens, split
1 medium onion, chopped
1 small green pepper, seeded and
    diced
1 3-oz. can sliced mushrooms
¼ tsp. marjoram
2 tbls. pimiento, diced

¾ cup long-grain rice, uncooked
½ cup dry Vermouth
½ cup chicken broth
salt and pepper to taste
2 tbls. butter or margarine,
    melted

If hens are frozen, thaw completely. Brown skin side in one tablespoon of the butter. Combine onion, green pepper, mushrooms with their liquor, marjoram, pimiento, Vermouth, broth, and rice; salt and pepper to taste; spoon into a buttered, shallow casserole. Lay cornish hens, skin side up, on top. Cover tightly with foil wrap. Bake at 350° for 45 minutes. Uncover; stir rice with fork; brush hens with remaining melted butter. Continue baking for 15 minutes, uncovered, or until rice is fluffy. Serves 4.

CORNISH GAME HENS WITH RICE STUFFING

2 1-lb. Cornish game hens
2 tbls. slivered almonds
⅓ cup uncooked rice
2 tbls. finely chopped onion
3 tbls. margarine or butter

1 cup water
1 chicken bouillon cube
½ tsp. salt
1 tsp. lemon juice
1 3-oz. can chopped mushrooms
    drained

Season game hens inside and out. Cook almonds, onions and ripe in butter in small saucepan 5 to 10 minutes, stirring frequently. Add water, bouillon cube, lemon juice, and salt. Reduce heat; cover and cook slowly about 20 to 25 minutes. Stir in the mushrooms. Lightly stuff birds with rice mixture. Place breast upon rack in shallow baking pan. Brush with melted margarine. Roast covered in hot oven 400° for 30 minutes. Uncover and roast 1 hour longer. Brush birds with melted margarine during last 15 minutes. Serves 2.

DUCKLING SUPREME

2 domestic ducklings
salt
apple juice

4-6 medium apples, cored and
    quartered
1 cup (or more) large, seedless raisins

Salt duck cavities; fill with apples and raisins. Roast duck, breast side up, covered, for 1 hour in 325° oven. Uncover; prick skin in many places to let fat run out. Remove about ⅓ of stuffing and place in pan around ducklings. Continue roasting uncovered for 1½ to 2 hours until ducks are tender and very brown. Baste with apple juice added to pan juices if ducks start to get too dry. Remove cooked ducks to a platter; keep warm. For gravy, push all drippings through a sieve; skim off fat. Adjust, if necessary, with flour and water or apple juice.

DUCK CASSEROLE

1 duck, about 4 lbs.
2 tbls. butter
¾ cup finely chopped onions
1 clove garlic, minced
2 cups chicken stock or bouillon

½ tsp. anise seeds, crushed
¼ tsp. cayenne
salt and pepper to taste
1 cup uncooked long-grain rice

Quarter the duck; brown in butter; place in Dutch oven. Pour off all but 1 tbls. fat from skillet; add onions and garlic; cook until onions have softened. Add stock to skillet; cook, stirring, to dissolve brown particles. Pour liquid over duck; salt and pepper to taste. Cover; cook, simmering, until duck is almost tender, about 1 hour. Skim off excess fat. Add anise seed, cayenne, and rice. Cook 20 to 30 minutes until rice is tender and liquid absorbed. Serves 4.

PHEASANT ORIENTAL

1 tbls. flour
1 large or 2 small pheasants, cut up
paprika
¼ cup soy sauce
2 tbls. honey
⅓ cup sliced water chestnuts

½ tsp. ground ginger
½ tsp. salt
¼ tsp. garlic powder
1 can (3-4 oz.) sliced mushrooms,
    drained

Shake flour in large size Brown-in-Bag and place in 12" x 8" x 2" baking dish. Season pheasant pieces with paprika and place in bag. In a small bowl, combine soy sauce, honey, ginger, salt, and garlic powder; pour over pheasant in bag. Add mushrooms and water chestnuts. Close bag with twist tie. Marinate in refrigerator 6 to 8 hours or overnight; turn bag once. When ready to cook, make 6 half-inch slits in top of bag. Cook in preheated 350° oven for 1 to 1¼ hours or until pheasant is tender.

PHEASANT IN CASSEROLE

1 pheasant, cut in serving pieces
1 cup flour
1 tbls. salt
1 tbls. paprika
½ tsp. pepper

2 tbls. butter
1 tbls. flour
1 cup light cream
1 cup sour cream

Combine flour, salt, pepper, and paprika in a bag. Add pheasant; shake in bag to coat. Remove pheasant from bag; shake off excess flour; brown in butter. Place pheasant in well greased casserole. Stir 1 tbls. flour into pan drippings, blend in sour cream and light cream. Pour mixture over pheasant; bake at 300° for 3 hours. Skim off any excess fat and stir sauce before serving. Serves 2 to 3.

ROAST TURKEY

Wash turkey and pat dry. If desired, rub cavity lightly with salt. Do not salt cavity if turkey is to be stuffed. Stuff turkey just before roasting, not ahead time. Fill wishbone area with stuffing first. Fasten neck skin to back with skewer. Fold wings across back with tips touching. Fill body cavity lightly. Tuck drumsticks under band of skin at tail or tie together with heavy string, then tie to tail. Heat oven to 325°. Place turkey breast side up on rack in open shallow roasting pan. Brush with shortening, oil or butter. Insert meat thermometer so tip is in thickest part of inside thigh muscle or thickest part of breast meat and does not touch bone. Do not add water. Do not cover.

Follow timetable for approximate total cooking time:

6 to 8 pounds	3 to 3½ hours	Internal temperature 185°
8 to 12 pounds	3½ to 4½ hours	Internal temperature 185°
12 to 16 pounds	4½ to 5½ hours	Internal temperature 185°
16 to 20 pounds	5½ to 6½ hours	Internal temperature 185°
20 to 24 pounds	6½ to 7 hours	Internal temperature 185°

BREAD STUFFING

9 cups soft bread cubes	**2 tsp. salt**
1 cup butter or margarine	**1½ tsp. sage leaves (crushed)**
1½ cups chopped celery	**½ tsp. pepper**
¾ cup minced onion	**1 tsp. thyme**

In large pan, cook and stir onion and celery in butter until onion is tender. Stir in about ⅓ of the bread cubes. Turn into deep bowl. Add remaining ingredients and toss. Stuff turkey just before roasting. 9 cups (enough for 12 lb. turkey).

Oyster Stuffing: Decrease bread cubes to 8 cups and add 1 pint oysters, drained and chopped, with the remaining ingredients.

CORN BREAD DRESSING (SOUTHERN STYLE)

4 cups crumbled cooked corn bread	**1 tbls. sage**
1 cup chopped onion	**salt and pepper to taste**
1 cup chopped celery	**chopped cooked turkey giblets**
¼ cup chopped parsley	**½ cup melted butter**
1 4-oz. can chopped mushrooms	**water from cooked giblets**

Combine corn bread, onions, celery, parsley, mushrooms and seasonings. At this point you may refrigerate the dressing until you are ready to stuff the turkey. Combine corn bread mixture and the giblets, melted butter. Add water from giblets and more hot water, if needed, until dressing is moistened but holds its shape when spooned. Stuff cavities of 10 to 12 pound turkey.

CHESTNUT STUFFING

1 lb. chestnuts	2 cups bread crumbs
¾ cup butter, melted	½ tsp. parsley, finely chopped
1 egg, lightly beaten	turkey liver, finely chopped
salt and pepper	

Cover chestnuts with boiling water; boil about 20 minutes until shell and skin can be easily removed. Place in blender a few at a time, blending until crumbly. Mix with bread crumbs and liver; add egg and butter. Add seasonings. If desired, ½ cup chopped celery and ¼ cup minced onion may be added to above.

MUSHROOM STUFFED BEEF

1½ or 2 lbs. butterflied steak	½ green pepper, chopped
2 tbls. margarine	1/8 tsp. sage or poultry dressing
½ lb. mushrooms, chopped or sliced	1/8 tsp. ground thyme
¼ cup chopped celery	1 tbls. flour
¼ cup chopped onion	¼ cup of sake, wine, beer or bouillon
salt and pepper to taste	

Melt butter in fry pan; sauté mushrooms until browned. Add remaining vegetables and sauté until tender. Blend in flour and herbs; thin with liquid until slightly wet. Place on one half of steak; fold other half over and secure with toothpicks. Place on roasting pan and roast at 325°, 20 minutes per pound. For backyard cooking, this can be broiled or pan fried. Turn once carefully.

SIRLOIN TIPS CHINOISE

1 qt. lobster sauce	1 large onion
2 lbs. sirloin beef tips	1 lb. mushrooms
1 cup raw rice, cooked	1 tbls. soy sauce
1 large green pepper	salt and pepper

Chop onions and pepper. Slice mushrooms. Sauté onions, pepper, mushrooms, and sirloin tips. Mix all ingredients in lobster sauce. Pour into casserole. Bake 45 minutes at 375°. Serves 8-10. Lobster sauce can be bought at any Chinese take-out shop.

BEEF-VEAL-KIDNEY CASSEROLE

4½ lbs. sirloin of beef in 1″ cubes
½ lb. veal in 1″ cubes
4 veal kidneys
3 lbs. onions, coarsely chopped
⅔ cup butter
⅔ cup flour
1 tbls. vinegar

5 cans beef consommé
¾ tsp. oregano
¾ tsp. thyme
½ tsp. hot pepper sauce
1 tsp. salt
½ tsp. pepper

Brown beef in butter; transfer to a deep casserole. Brown veal chunks; set aside. Brown onions; add to beef in casserole. Melt butter in same skillet; blend in flour; gradually add consommé, stirring to form a smooth sauce, scraping bottom of pan to blend in all the brown bits. Season with oregano, thyme, salt, pepper, and hot sauce. Pour sauce over onions and beef in casserole. Simmer veal kidneys until tender in enough water to cover, to which vinegar has been added. Cool slightly. Cut in thin slices, removing membrane; add to casserole. Bake for 45 minutes in a 350° oven. Add browned veal cubes; bake one hour longer. Serve over buttered noodles sprinkled with caraway seeds. Serves 12.

BEEF AND PEPPERS ORIENTAL

1½ lbs. sirloin or flank steak, cut
    diagonally into thin strips
1 clove garlic, minced
½ tsp. ginger
1 tbls. soy sauce
1 tsp. cooking oil
2 tsps. cornstarch
2 sliced Bermuda (or sweet) onions
2 green peppers, cut in strips

3 tomatoes, seeded and quartered
1 tsp. sugar
1 cup canned beef bouillon
1 tbls. cornstarch
1 tsp. soy sauce
¼ cup cold water
2 tbls. sherry
oil

Combine ginger, garlic, 1 tablespoon soy sauce, 1 teaspoon oil, and 2 teaspoons cornstarch; add beef strips; toss to cover. Sauté small amounts of meat in hot oil quickly until done; remove from pan and keep warm. Add oil to pan; heat; add onions and green peppers; cook, stirring, for 2 to 3 minutes. Add bouillon and bring to a boil. Blend 1 tablespoon of cornstarch with ¼ cup of cold water; add to hot mixture; add 1 teaspoon sugar and 1 teaspoon soy sauce; simmer 2 to 3 minutes. Add meat and sherry. If not to be served immediately, may be refrigerated or frozen at this point. Add tomatoes one or two minutes before serving. Serves 6.

SWISS STEAK

½ lb. bottom round   ketchup
1 envelope onion soup mix, cup size   1 to 2 medium onions, sliced
flour, salt, and pepper

Sprinkle both sides of steak with mixture of flour, salt, and pepper, pounding mixture into meat with the back of a heavy knife. Place steak on heavy foil, or double thickness of regular foil. Cover steak liberally with ketchup. Add a layer of sliced onions; sprinkle with onion soup mix. Seal pack, envelope style, tightly; place in shallow pan. Bake at 350° for 1½ hours. Serves 2.

BEWITCHED SWISS STEAK

1½ lbs. top round steak, cut 1-inch   1½ cups canned tomatoes
  thick   ½ tsp. basil
1 tsp. dry mustard   2 tbls. Worcestershire sauce
½ cup flour   1 tbls. brown sugar
1 cup sliced onions   ¼ cup red Burgundy
2 carrots, sliced   5 (or more) mushrooms, sliced
salt and pepper

Mix dry mustard and flour; pound into both sides of steak with a meat mallet; season with salt and pepper to taste. Brown meat in a little fat on both sides. Place meat in a small roaster or covered casserole. Add onions, carrots, tomatoes, basil, Worcestershire, sugar, Burgundy, and mushrooms. Cook, covered, at 325° for 3 hours or until tender. If liquid evaporates, add more wine. Serves 4.

BOEUF BOURGUIGNON

2 lbs. cubed beef   1 clove garlic
4 carrots, sliced 1″ thick   1 cup tomato sauce
1 cup celery, sliced in ½″ pieces   3 tbls. minute tapioca
2 onions, sliced ¼″ thick   ½ cup Burgundy wine
2 cups canned whole tomatoes,   1 cup water chestnuts, sliced
  drained   2 4-oz. cans mushrooms
1 tbls. sugar   1 can small whole potatoes

Mix all but last three ingredients in large casserole, leaving at least 2″ at top so mixture will not bubble over. Cover; cook in 250° oven for 4 hours. Add water chestnuts, mushrooms, and potatoes; cook for 1 hour more. Serves 6.

HERBED BEEF STEW

¼ cup butter
4 lbs. beef chuck cut into 1½" cubes
1 lb. sliced mushrooms
6 yellow onions, peeled & chopped
2 cloves garlic, crushed
1 tbls. salt
1 tsp. dried dill
¾ tsp. basil
½ tsp. thyme

½ tsp. savory
¼ tsp. pepper
2 crushed bay leaves
1 can beef consommé (10½ ozs.)
1 lb. small white onions
  peeled
1 bunch carrots, cut in 2" chunks
2 1-lb. 13-oz. cans tomatoes
6 tbls. flour
¼ cup water

Melt butter in a large kettle and brown meat. Add mushrooms, onions, garlic, herbs, bay leaves and salt and pepper. Sauté slowly, stirring occasionally until onions and mushrooms are tender. Now add consommé and tomatoes and simmer 1½ hours until meat is tender. Add white onions and carrots. Cover kettle and cook 45 minutes more until vegetables are done. Mix 6 tbls flour with ¼ cup cold water until smooth and add to meat mixture, stirring constantly. Continue to stir until gravy thickens. Serve in a large tureen with a garnish of parsley or frozen peas.

BEEF BURGUNDY

3 lbs. beef round steak, ¼" thick
¼ cup flour
4 tbls. margarine
½ cup chopped onions
1 tbls. finely chopped parsley
1 large clove garlic (crushed)

1 bay leaf
salt and pepper
1 6-oz. can mushrooms
1 cup Burgundy
1 cup water

Cut steak into bite-size cubes; shake in a bag with the flour to coat. Brown pieces in margarine in skillet. Remove from heat and add the remaining ingredients. Heat mixture to boiling. Reduce heat and simmer. covered, about 1 hour or till meat is tender. Remove bay leaf before serving. Serve over rice or hot cooked noodles. Serves 6 to 8.

NOODLE CASSEROLE

½ lb. egg noodles, cooked and drained
1 lb. ground chuck
2 8-oz. cans tomato sauce
1 cup cottage cheese
¼ cup sour cream
⅓ cup minced green onions
1 tbls. minced green pepper
2 tbls. melted butter or margarine
1 8-oz. pkg. softened cream cheese

Brown meat; stir in tomato sauce; remove from heat. Combine cottage cheese, cream cheese, sour cream, onion, and green pepper. In a 2-quart casserole, spread half the noodles; cover with cheese mixture; then the remaining noodles. Pour melted butter over noodles; then pour tomato-meat sauce mix over all. Bake at 375° for 45 minutes. Serves six.

ITALIAN STUFFED RICE CASSEROLE

1 lb. ground beef
6 sweet Italian sausages, sliced
oil optional
1 small onion diced
1 large can Italian tomatoes
   with liquid, crush in blender
1 clove garlic minced
1 (6-oz.) can tomato paste
1 tsp. salt
½ tsp. black pepper
¼ tsp. oregano
½ tsp. basil

Brown beef and sausages in a large skillet. Use a little oil if needed. Drain fat. Add the remaining ingredients and simmer over low heat 1½ hours.

Cheese Filling

1 large container Ricotta (2 lbs.)
½ cup grated Mozarella cheese
4 eggs
1 tsp. parsley
¼ cup grated Parmesan cheese
1 tsp. salt
½ tsp. pepper
1 lb. box rice

Combine ingredients in large bowl. Cook a 1 lb. box of rice. Spoon a little meat sauce over bottom of a 9″ x 13″ x 2″ pan. Put in half of rice, half of cheese and a layer of meat sauce. Repeat all the layers. Bake at 350° for 45 minutes. Serve with any remaining meat sauce. Serves 12.

BEEF LIVER TERIYAKI

1 lb. beef liver	1 large onion, sliced
¼ cup flour	¼ cup water
¼ cup soy sauce	3 tbls. vegetable oil
2 tbls. sugar	pepper, garlic salt

Cut liver into small strips. Roll strips in flour on wax paper. Combine soy sauce, water, and sugar. Heat oil in large skillet; add onion, sauté 1 minute. Add liver strips, brown quickly, stirring constantly. Lower heat, stir in soy sauce mixture. Cook until thickened. Add pepper & garlic salt. Serve over rice. Serves 2 to 4.

JOHNNY MAZETTA

2 cups chopped green peppers	2 4-oz. cans sliced mushrooms with liquid
1 cup chopped celery	
2 cups chopped onion	1 can tomato soup (10½ oz.)
2 lbs. ground beef	2 or 3 cans (8 oz.) tomato sauce
1 lb. ground pork	1 pound bread noodles
1 cup butter or margarine	2 garlic cloves, crushed
2 tsps. salt	2 cups grated sharp cheese (½ lb.)
½ cup sliced stuffed olives	

In large skillet sauté pepper, celery, onion, garlic and meat in hot butter. Add salt. Reduce heat; cook 5 minutes. Stir in olives, mushrooms with liquid, soup, and sauce. Cook 5 minutes. Cook noodles according to box directions; drain and rinse. Turn noodles into large roasting pan (14" x 10" x 2½" or larger). Add sauce and stir gently until well mixed. Sprinkle grated cheese on top. Bake at 350° for 35 minutes. Delicious made ahead and freezes well. Serves 12.

SAUSAGE BEEF CASSEROLE

6 sweet Italian sausages
1 lb. beef chuck, cut in 1" cubes
1 large onion, sliced
2 cloves garlic, minced
2 medium green peppers, seeded
   and cut in eighths
4 medium potatoes, peeled &
   quartered

2 cans red kidney beans, drained
1 tsp. basil
½ tsp. salt
¼ tsp. pepper
2 beef bouillon cubes dissolved in
   1 cup boiling water

Brown sausages well; cut in thirds; place in 2½-3 quart casserole. Drain fat, reserving 2 tbls. Brown beef in 1 tbls. fat; then add to casserole. Cook onions and garlic in remaining 1 tbls. fat till tender; add green pepper; cook 1 minute. Place in casserole, add potatoes and beans. Sprinkle with seasonings, mix lightly. Pour bouillon over; cover and cook at 350° for one hour and 15 minutes until beef and potatoes are tender. Serves 4-6.

MEAT LOAF WELLINGTON

Pastry:
4 cups flour
1¼ cups butter, at room
   temperature

2 eggs
1 tsp. salt
½ cup cold water

Blend flour, butter, and salt in large bowl; work with hands until smooth. Add eggs; add water until pastry is of rolling consistency. Chill one hour.

Meatloaf:
1½ lbs. lean beef
¾ lb. mushrooms, finely chopped
½ cup minced onion
¾ cup soft bread crumbs

⅓ cup ketchup
1½ tsps. salt
2 eggs, slightly beaten
¼ tsp. black pepper
⅓ lb. liver sausage

Combine all ingredients except liver sausage in large bowl; shape into oval loaf. Bake on cookie sheet in 350° preheated oven for ½ hour. Cool; drain off fat. Roll out ½ of pastry to size 1" larger than loaf; place loaf in center. Make paste of liver sausage and spread over meat loaf. Roll out reserved pastry to large enough rectangle to encase meat loaf. Seal edges to bottom pastry with water. Cut decorative leaves or other designs from scraps of pastry. Place on top of loaf. Brush over crust with beaten egg. Bake at 400° for 30 minutes or until lightly browned. Serves 6.

ZUCCHINI MEATLOAF

1½ lbs. lean ground beef
½ cup dry bread crumbs
⅔ cup tomato paste
2 eggs, beaten
½ cup chopped onions
¼ cup chopped green pepper
¾ tsp. salt, dash of pepper

¼ cup grated Parmesan or Romano
pinch of dried parsley and basil
2 tbls. olive or corn oil
1 clove garlic, crushed or pinch of
   garlic powder
2 or 3 medium zucchini, sliced ⅓" thick
tomato sauce
Romano cheese, grated

Combine bread crumbs, beef, tomato paste, eggs, onion, green pepper, salt, pepper, grated cheese, parsley, and basil in a large bowl; mix well. Heat oil in skillet; add garlic; add zucchini. Sauté, uncovered, over medium heat until tender - crisp, about 10 minutes, stirring occasionally. (If using garlic powder, sprinkle on zucchini while cooking.) Put half meat mixture into greased 2-quart casserole; cover with zucchini; top with remaining meat mixture. If desired, top may now be spread with a little tomato sauce and sprinkled with Romano cheese. Bake 1 hour in a preheated 350° oven. Cool several minutes before serving. Serves 6 to 8.

ZUCCHINI BEEF CASSEROLE

1 qt. sliced fresh zucchini
1 lb. lean ground beef
1 cup chopped onions
1 clove garlic, crushed
1 tsp. each salt and basil
½ tsp. oregano

¼ tsp. pepper
2 cups cooked rice
1 8-oz. can tomato sauce
1 cup cottage cheese
1 egg, beaten
1 cup grated Cheddar cheese

Cook zucchini in boiling salted water 2 to 3 minutes; drain well; set aside. Sauté ground meat, onions, garlic, and seasonings until onions are transparent. Stir rice and tomato sauce into meat mixture. In another bowl, blend cottage cheese and egg. Arrange half of the zucchini slices in a buttered shallow 2-qt. casserole. Spoon on meat-rice mixture. Spread cottage cheese over meat mixture. Top with remaining zucchini and sprinkle with Cheddar cheese. Bake uncovered at 350° for 20 to 25 minutes or until bubbly. Serves 6.

CURRIED LAMB

3 lbs. lamb shoulder, cubed
2 cloves garlic, minced
4 large onions, sliced
4 apples, cored, pared, and
   coarsely chopped
4 tbls. curry powder
4 tbls. brown sugar
⅔ cup nuts, pecans or walnuts

2 cups water or stock
½ cup butter, melted
4 tbls. raisins
2 tbls. Worcestershire sauce
1 tbls. salt
2 lemons, thinly sliced
4 tbls. shredded coconut

Brown meat, onions, and garlic in butter. Add apples and curry; cook for 5 minutes. Add water or stock; add remaining ingredients except nuts. Cover; simmer for 1 hour. Add nuts; simmer 10 minutes more. Sprinkle additional coconut over each serving. Serves 8. (Leftover lamb may be used.)

LAMB CHOPS SUPREME

12 loin lamb chops
4 green peppers
1 6-oz. box wild rice
1 onion, chopped

4 tbls. butter or margarine
½ lb. mushrooms, sliced
flour, salt, pepper, and garlic salt
mint jelly

Mix flour and seasonings; dredge chops with mixture. Brown chops in a skillet on both sides using half of the butter. Remove chops to a large, shallow casserole. Slice three ½" to ¾" rings from each green pepper; remove core and seeds; chop remaining green pepper coarsely. Drop pepper rings (there should be 12) in boiling water; boil for 5 minutes; drain. Place a ring on each lamb chop. Add remaining butter to skillet; sauté onions and chopped peppers until onions are transparent; add sliced mushrooms; cook for 3 minutes. Cook rice according to package directions; add to sautéed vegetables; mix well. Fill green pepper rings with mixture. Bake casserole, covered, at 325° for 40 minutes. Uncover; bake 20 minutes longer. For the last 5 minutes of cooking time, spoon 1 teaspoon of mint jelly on each chop for garnish. Serves 6.

GIGOT À LA MOUTARDE (ROAST LAMB)

1 6-lb. leg of lamb
Coating:
½ cup Dijon-type prepared mustard   1 tsp. ground rosemary or thyme
2 tbls. soy sauce   ¼ tsp. ground ginger
1 clove mashed garlic   2 tbls. olive oil

Blend together all coating ingredients except olive oil; add oil by droplets, using medium speed of mixer, to make a mayonnaise-like cream. Paint lamb with mixture; set on rack in roasting pan in oven. Let set several hours — if possible — before cooking. Roast at 350° for 1¼ to 1½ hours or until done.

PORK CHOPS IN SAUERKRAUT

8 lean loin pork chops   2 1-lb. cans applesauce
2 large onions, finely chopped   1 1-lb. 14 oz. can sauerkraut

Trim fat from chops. Brown lightly on both sides in a very hot skillet; remove from heat. Drain sauerkraut thoroughly; spread over bottom of large, rectangular baking dish. Place chops in single layer on top of sauerkraut. Cook chopped onion until transparent and lightly browned in pork drippings in skillet. Add applesauce to onions; mix well; spread over chops, covering completely. Bake at 350° for 1½ hours or until chops are done. Serves 4 to 8.

DRUNKEN PORK CHOPS

6 thick pork chops (¾" to 1")   1 sliced onion
1 can beer   6 tbls. brown sugar
½ cup ketchup   salt & pepper

Brown pork chops in own fat. Place in low baking dish. Sprinkle each chop with 1 tbls. brown sugar. Place slice of onion **under** each chop. Mix beer and ketchup and pour over chops. Bake at 350° for 1¼ hours or until tender. Serves 3 to 6.

A DOLLS' PARTY

The cloth laid, the table set with their best hand-painted china, the porcelain-faced dolls wait patiently on their Windsor chairs for the tea ceremony to commence.

Dolls' Tea Party

Cinnamon Toast

Cucumber Sandwiches

Weary Willie Cake

Cookies

Cambric Tea

GOURMET PORK CHOPS

6 loin pork chops
2 tbls. flour
1 tsp. salt
dash of pepper
1 10½-oz. can cream of
  mushroom soup

¾ cup of water
½ tsp. ground ginger
¼ tsp. rosemary, crushed
½ cup sour cream
1 can French fried onion rings

Trim fat from chops; coat in mixture of flour, salt and pepper; brown both sides in hot fat. Place in one layer in baking dish. Combine soup, sour cream, water, ginger and rosemary; pour over chops; sprinkle with one-half of onions. Cover; bake at 350° for 50 minutes or until meat is tender. Uncover; sprinkle with remaining onion rings. Continue baking uncovered for 10 minutes. Serves 3 to 6.

PORK AND EGGPLANT FRICASSEE

¼ cup flour
3 lbs. pork, cubed
3 tbls. oil
1 cup chicken broth
2 tsps. salt
2 green peppers, seeds and
  membrane removed

1 tsp. oregano
1 tsp. thyme
¼ tsp. sage
¼ tsp. freshly ground pepper
2 medium eggplants, cubed
1 jar pimiento, drained

Place flour and pork in bag; shake thoroughly to coat pork. Heat oil in heavy skillet or Dutch oven; brown pork. Add broth and spices; cover; simmer for 1 hour. Cut green peppers and pimiento into chunks or strips. Add eggplant xnd peppers to skillet; simmer 15 minutes. Add pimiento. Serves 6 to 8.

PORK CHOPS WITH DRESSING

4 loin pork chops
¼ cup butter
¼ cup chopped onions
¾ tsp. salt
1/8 tsp. thyme
4 cups soft bread cubes

1/8 tsp. cloves
2 tbls. sugar
¼ cup raisins
¼ cup water or cider
1½ cups sliced tart apples

Brown chops slowly on both sides. Set aside. Add butter to drippings and cook until clear. Mix all ingredients (except chops) and arrange in flat casserole. Place chops on top. Bake, covered, in 350° oven for about 1 hour. Remove cover last 10 minutes to finish browning. Serves 4.

PORK ROAST (MARINATED)

1½ tsps. salt
1½ tsps. whole allspice
1 tsp. whole cloves
½ tsp. black pepper
½ tsp. ground marjoram
½ tsp. ground sage
1 crumbled bay leaf

1 tbls. slivered lemon rind
2 tbls. fresh lemon juice
2 10½-oz. cans beef bouillon
4 to 5 lb. loin of pork roast
1 tbls. fat
½ cup sliced onion
½ cup sliced carrots

Heat together the first 10 ingredients to boiling point. Pour over pork. Cool. Marinate 24 hours in refrigerator; turning several times. Remove meat from marinade; reserve marinade. Brown meat on all sides in heavy pan. Add marinade and vegetables. Cover; bring to simmer; simmer 2 hours or until meat is tender or bake in covered roasting pan in preheated, slow oven, 325°, 3 hours. Remove meat and strain gravy. Thicken with 1½ tablespoons flour for each cup of gravy. Serves 6 to 8.

PANZETTA

1 whole veal rib cage
paprika
butter
1 small carton Ricotta

¼ cup parsley, preferably Italian
¼ cup grated Parmesan
2 eggs, slightly beaten

Have butcher cut pocket in veal; be **very** sure skin is not punctured. Mix Ricotta, parsley, Parmesan, and eggs. Stuff pocket, leaving some space. Secure open end well. Cover veal with butter; liberally sprinkle with paprika. Bake at 325° for 1 hour or until done. Serve by cutting between ribs. Serves 6 to 8. Variation: add chopped spinach to stuffing.

VEAL PAPRIKA

1½ lbs. veal cutlets
2 tbls. flour
salt and pepper
1 tbls. paprika

2 tbls. butter
1 cup hot water
1 cup sweet or sour cream
4 to 6 ozs. noodles, cooked

Roll veal in flour seasoned with salt, pepper, and paprika. Place in refrigerator for 2 hours. Melt butter in skillet; add veal and brown on both sides. Add 1 cup of hot water; cover; simmer 1½ hours or until tender. Remove veal to a hot platter; surround with noodles. Add cream to pan drippings; stir until hot; pour over veal and noodles. Serves 4.

VEAL PICCATA

4 veal scallops, pounded thin
flour, salt, and pepper
6 tbls. butter

2 tbls. oil
3 tbls. lemon juice
2 tbls. parsley, chopped

Dust scallops with mixture of salt, pepper, and flour. Heat 4 tablespoons butter plus oil in a skillet over medium heat until bubbly. Quickly brown scallops, about 2 minutes on each side; remove to warm platter. Add lemon juice and parsley to skillet; remove from heat and swirl in the remaining butter. Pour sauce over scallops; garnish with lemon slices and parsley. Serves 2.

CURRY OF VEAL WITH BRAZIL NUTS

3½ lbs. veal, cubed
24 Brazil nuts, cut in half
3 bunches celery (4 cups), sliced thin
1 stick margarine or butter
4 tbls. flour

1 cup milk or water, or ½ each
1 cup white wine
½ tsp. curry or to taste
salt and pepper

Cover celery with salted water and simmer 2 to 3 minutes, so still quite crunchy; drain. Sauté veal in margarine. Make sauce of 4 tablespoons of margarine, 4 tablespoons of flour, and the 2 cups of liquid. Sauce should be fairly thin; add more liquid if necessary. Add seasonings. Pour over veal; add celery. Mix together and place in casserole. Cook covered at 350° for 45 minutes to 1½ hours, depending on size of pieces of veal. Fifteen minutes before serving, add nuts which have been sautéed in 1 tablespoon of margarine. Serves 12.

MOLDED CORNED BEEF

1 12-oz. can corned beef
1 pkg. lemon gelatin
½ envelope plain gelatin
¼ cup cold water
1½ cups hot water
2 tbls. lemon juice
1 cup finely cut celery

2 tbls. minced onion
½ green pepper, finely chopped
1 cup mayonnaise
¼ cup sweet pickle relish
1 small jar pimientos, chopped
3 hard-boiled eggs, chopped

Soak plain gelatin in cold water; dissolve lemon gelatin in hot water; mix the plain and lemon gelatins; add lemon juice; cool. Add chopped celery, minced onion, green pepper, and corned beef which has been broken up into small pieces. Fold in the mayonnaise, pickle relish, pimientos, and eggs. Mold in 8" x 8" dish overnight. Garnish with sour cream and sliced olives. Serves 8.

VENISON STEW

4 lbs. venison, cut into 1½" to 2" cubes
3 cans beef bouillon
3 soup cans Burgundy wine
2 large or 4 small bay leaves
salt and pepper to taste

12 to 16 medium onions
12 to 16 carrots, cut in 1" lengths
12 to 16 small to medium potatoes, halved or quartered
1 large can mushrooms

Brown venison cubes in a little oil in a large kettle; add bouillon, wine, bay leaves, salt, and pepper. Simmer, covered, 2 hours. Add onions; simmer ½ hour. Add carrots; simmer ½ hour. Add potatoes; simmer 1 hour or until vegetables are done. Add mushrooms. Salt and pepper to taste. Gravy may be thickened with flour or cornstarch as desired. Serves 6 to 8.

EGGS SCRAMBLED WITH LOBSTER OR CRAB

3 tbls. butter
8 eggs
2 tbls. sour cream
3 tbls. dry Vermouth

½ tsp. salt
1 cup cooked lobster or crabmeat
½ cup whole, shelled shrimp, cooked
1 to 2 tbls. sliced almonds

Melt butter in wide, shallow serving dish over direct heat. Blend sour cream with Vermouth; beat in 6 of the eggs. Pour mixture into butter, which should be sizzling; cook, stirring gently from bottom of dish as eggs begin to set. Add lobster or crab, shrimp, and almonds. Continue cooking until eggs are set. Break the remaining 2 eggs into a small bowl; mix very slightly with a fork. Pour over eggs in pan to glaze all. Cook a few seconds longer to allow glaze to set. Serves 4 to 6.

EGGS EIFFEL TOWER

4 slices dry toast or rusks
1 4½-oz. can deviled ham
¾ cup shredded processed cheese
6 eggs, separated
¼ tsp. cream of tartar

10 drops bottled hot pepper sauce
dash of salt
1 tsp. prepared mustard
butter

Cut toast to fit into bottoms of four 6-ounce custard cups. Butter the toast; spread each slice with 1 tablespoon of deviled ham; place in cup; sprinkle with 1 tablespoon of cheese. Beat whites of eggs with cream of tartar, hot pepper sauce, and salt until soft peaks form; gradually add mustard, beating until stiff. Place a heaping tablespoon of egg-white mixture on top of cheese in cup; top with a whole egg yolk. Dot egg yolk layer with about ½ tablespoon each of deviled ham, broken into bits. Sprinkle with 1 tablespoon each of cheese. Top with enough of egg-white mixture to cover. Repeat layers of ham and cheese. Top with egg whites piled high. Bake at 325° for 30 minutes and whites are golden. Serves 4. (Remaining 2 egg yolks may be added to two of towers or reserved for other use.)

SWISS CHEESE QUICHE — A BASIC RECIPE

1 9-inch pie crust, uncooked	4 eggs
1 tbls. butter or margarine, softened	¾ tsp. salt
2 cups heavy or whipping cream	¼ lb. (1 cup) shredded Swiss

Spread pie crust with softened butter or margarine. In medium bowl, mix cream, eggs, and salt until well blended; stir in cheese. Pour mixture into pie crust. Bake in preheated 425° oven 15 minutes; reduce heat to 325° and bake 35 minutes longer or until knife inserted in center comes out clean. Serves 6. To reheat; cover quiche with foil; bake at 325° for 40 minutes or until heated through.

SHERRIED-CRAB QUICHE

pie crust and basic recipe	2 tbls. dry Sherry
3 tbls. butter or margarine	¼ tsp. salt
2 tbls. minced green onion	1/8 tsp. cayenne
12 ozs. crabmeat, fresh or frozen	

Over medium heat, melt butter in skillet; add onions; cook until tender. Thaw crabmeat if frozen. Thoroughly drain crabmeat; stir into onions; add to basic recipe. Add Sherry, salt, and cayenne. Pour into pie crust. Bake as for basic recipe. Serves 6.

BROCCOLI QUICHE

pie crust and basic recipe	1 10-oz. pkg. frozen chopped broccoli
2 tbls. butter or margarine	1/8 tsp. ground nutmeg
2 tbls. minced green onion	¼ tsp. pepper

Defrost and thoroughly drain the broccoli. Over medium heat, melt butter in skillet; add onions; cook until tender. Stir broccoli into onions; stir mixture into basic recipe. Add nutmeg and pepper. Pour into pie crust. Bake as for basic recipe. Serves 6.

SPINACH-MUSHROOM QUICHE

pie crust for 2-crust pie
6 tbls. butter or margarine
1 lb. mushrooms, thinly sliced
¼ cup minced onions
2 10-oz. pkgs. frozen, chopped
  spinach
6 eggs, lightly beaten

1½ cups heavy or whipping cream
1 cup milk
2 tbls. flour
1 tsp. salt
1/8 tsp. cayenne
1/8 tsp. ground nutmeg
½ lb. grated Swiss (2 cups)

Prepare pie crust; roll dough into 17″ x 15″ rectangle; use to line a 13″ x 9″ shallow baking dish; crimp edges. Cover and refrigerate. Melt 2 tablespoons butter in a skillet; cook mushrooms and onions until tender; remove from heat. Thoroughly drain the spinach; add to mushrooms and onions. In saucepan, melt 4 tablespoons of butter; remove from heat. Whisk in eggs and cream; add milk, flour, salt, cayenne; and nutmeg. Combine thoroughly. Spoon spinach mixture evenly onto crust; sprinkle with Swiss cheese. Pour egg mixture over cheese. Bake in preheated 425° oven 15 minutes. Reduce heat to 325°. Bake 40 minutes longer or until knife inserted in center comes out clean. Serves 12.

HAMBURGER QUICHE

1 lb. ground beef
1 cup chopped onion
1 cup mayonnaise
1 cup milk

1 cup grated Swiss or Cheddar
4 eggs, lightly beaten
2 tbls. flour
2 pie shells, partially baked (7″ or 8″)

Bake pie shells for 5 to 10 minutes. Crumble hamburger and brown with onion in a skillet. Blend together the remaining ingredients; stir into meat mixture. Pour half into each pie shell. Bake at 350° for 40 minutes. Sprinkle lightly with paprika; garnish with parsley. Serves 6 to 8.

OYSTER AND MUSHROOM RAREBIT

½ lb. sliced mushrooms
1½ doz. oysters
4 tbls. butter
dash of salt

2 tbls. flour
1½ cups light cream
3 cups grated cheese
1 tsp. Worcestershire

Sauté in 1 tablespoon of butter the mushrooms until golden brown. Remove from pan and set aside. Add oysters to pan with second tablespoon of butter; heat just until edges begin to curl. In a saucepan, melt remaining 2 tablespoons of butter; add flour; cook, stirring, until smooth. Add cream slowly; continue stirring until mixture bubbles. Add cheese; heat gently until melted and blended into sauce. Add Worcestershire; salt to taste. Add oysters and mushrooms. Serve on toast points. Serves 2 to 4.

ITALIAN FRITTATA

4 slices bacon, crisply cooked
1 cup chopped zucchini
⅓ cup chopped green pepper
⅓ cup chopped onion
1¼ cups cooked small shell
   macaroni, drained (½ cup
   uncooked)

½ tsp. celery salt
½ to 1 tsp. dried oregano, crushed
¼ tsp. pepper
6 eggs, beaten
¼ cup grated Romano
Dairy sour cream or chili sauce

Cook zucchini, green pepper, and onion in an 8″ ovenproof skillet to which 2 tablespoons of bacon drippings have been added. Stir in cooked macaroni, celery salt, oregano, pepper, and bacon which has been crumbled. Preheat broiler to a moderate temperature. Pour eggs evenly over zucchini mixture. Cook over medium heat until bottom is set and lightly browned (about 5 minutes). Broil about 2 minutes about 3″ below heat. Sprinkle with Romano; broil 1 or 2 minutes more until top is set and lightly browned. Serve in wedges with sour cream or chili sauce. Serves 4 to 6.

CREAMED EGGS AND ASPARAGUS

1 10-oz. pkg. frozen asparagus,
   cooked
3 tbls. butter
3 tbls. flour
1¾ cups milk

salt and pepper
½ cup shredded processed sharp cheese
5 hard-cooked eggs, sliced
paprika

Melt butter; add flour; cook until smooth. Add milk; cook, stirring, until thick; season with salt and pepper. Add cheese, stirring until melted and blended. Fold in the sliced, hard-cooked eggs gently. Spoon into a lightly greased 9″-square pan; arrange asparagus spears decoratively on top. Sprinkle with paprika. Keep warm until served. Serve on hot toast. Serves 4.

FRENCH OMELET SOUFFLÉ

1 tsp. butter or margarine
1 tsp. sugar
4 eggs, separated

3 tbls. sugar
1 tbls. cornstarch
3 tbls. sherry

Preheat oven to 400°. Butter the bottom of a 1-quart casserole; sprinkle with 1 teaspoon of sugar. Beat egg yolks with 3 tablespoons sugar and cornstarch until thick and light in color; stir in sherry. Beat egg whites until very stiff; fold into egg yolq mixture. Pour into casserole. Slash top in four places. Bake 15 to 20 minutes or until golden brown. Serve immediately. Serves 4. Serve for lunch with a salad; serve with strawberry sauce for dessert.

CHEESE-RICE SOUFFLÉ

½ cup water	1 cup grated sharp Cheddar
1 chicken bouillon cube	1 cup milk
½ cup cooked rice	½ tsp. salt
4 eggs, separated	1 tsp. grated onion
¼ cup butter or margarine, melted	¼ cup unsifted flour

Bring water to a boil; add bouillon cube and dissolve. Stir in the cooked rice; cover; remove from heat; let stand 5 minutes. Beat egg yolks slightly; beat egg whites until stiff. In saucepan, stir flour into melted butter; cook until smooth; gradually add milk. Cook and stir over medium heat until mixture thickens. Stir in cheese, salt, onion, and rice mixture. Stir in beaten egg yolks. Fold in the beaten egg whites. Pour into greased 1½-quart casserole. Bake at 325° for 50 minutes or until firm. Serves 4.

ASPARAGUS SANDWICH PUFF

6 bread slices	¼ cup salad dressing
6 slices processed American cheese	¼ tsp. salt
24 asparagus spears, cooked	dash of pepper
3 egg yolks	3 egg whites, stiffly beaten

Toast bread slices on one side; place a slice of cheese on untoasted side of each bread slice. Broil 1 to 2 minutes to partially melt the cheese. Remove from heat; place 4 hot asparagus spears on top of each cheese slice. Beat egg yolks until thick; stir in salad dressing, salt, and pepper. Fold in the beaten egg whites. Divide mixture evenly and pile on top of the asparagus. Bake at 350° about 12 to 13 minutes, or until egg mixture is set. Serves 6.

HEARTY GERMAN OMELET

¼ cup butter or margarine	6 eggs
2 cups cubed raw potatoes	¾ tsp. salt
¼ cup finely chopped onion	dash of pepper
1 cup diced ham	2 tbls. light cream
¼ cup chopped parsley	½ cup shredded Cheddar

Melt butter in large skillet; add potatoes and onion; cover; cook over medium heat, stirring occasionally, until potatoes are tender and golden brown, about 20 minutes. Add ham; cook a few minutes until lightly browned. Sprinkle with parsley. Blend well the eggs, salt, pepper, and light cream; pour over potato mixture. Reduce heat and cook until eggs are almost set, about 10 minutes. Slip a spatula around edge of pan occasionaly to allow egg mixture to flow to bottom of pan. Sprinkle with cheese; cover until cheese melts. Serves 6.

BREAKFAST CASSEROLE

3 medium tomatoes, peeled
3 tbls. butter
1 small onion, sliced
½ cup green pepper, diced
½ clove garlic, mashed
½ lb. lean ground beef
¼ lb. lean pork sausage meat

2 tbls. flour
½ tsp. salt
½ tsp. chili powder
dash of pepper
6 eggs
¼ lb. Cheddar, cut in strips

Halve the tomatoes; discard seeds; scoop out pulp and set aside. Melt butter in a large skillet; add onion, green pepper, and garlic; cook until vegetables are tender. Add beef and sausage and tomato pulp; cook over medium heat, stirring, for 10 minutes. Combine flour, salt, and chili powder; sprinkle over meat; mix well. Cook 3 to 4 minutes until thickened. Turn mixture into an 8″ x 12″ baking dish. Arrange tomato shells, open side up, over meat. Carefully crack an egg into each tomato shell; cross 2 strips of cheese over top of each filled tomato. Bake at 350° for 20 to 25 minutes. Serves 6.

HAM-BROCCOLI-CHEESE STRATA

6 slices firm white bread, crusts
  removed
8 ozs. Cheddar cheese, grated
1 pkg. frozen baby broccoli spears,
  defrosted and drained
2 cups diced ham

3 slightly beaten eggs
1¾ cups milk
1 tbls. instant minced onion
¼ tsp. salt
1/8 tsp. dry mustard

Cut circles, triangles, or other designs from bread and set aside. Break up remaining bread and scatter over bottom of a greased 12″ x 10″ casserole. Cover bread with 6 ounces of cheese. Spread with well drained broccoli and the ham. Decorate with reserved bread circles. Combine remaining ingredients and pour over all. Sprinkle with 2 ounces of cheese. Cover and refrigerate for at least 6 hours. Bake uncovered for 55 minutes at 325°. Serves 6. May use turkey instead of ham or half of each.

SOUFFLÉ SANDWICH WITH CRABMEAT

10 slices thick white bread
butter
garlic salt
¼ to ½ lb. grated Swiss
Parmesan

3 eggs
1½ cups liquid - 1 jigger sherry plus
    milk to make 1½ cups
1 large can or ½ lb. crabmeat,
    shredded

Remove crusts from bread; butter one side and sprinkle with garlic salt. Place half the bread, buttered side down, in a large, shallow, greased baking dish. Sprinkle grated cheese over bread; spread crabmeat over that. Place remaining bread on top, buttered side down. Beat together eggs, milk, and salt; pour over bread layers. Sprinkle generously with Parmesan. Refrigerate overnight or at least 8 hours, covered. Remove from refrigerator 2 to 3 hours before baking. Bake at 325° for 1 hour. Serves 8. Small shrimp may be substituted for crabmeat.

MOCK SOUFFLÉ WITH SAUTERNE

6 slices thick white bread
½ cup chicken bouillon
½ lb. grated Swiss
1 cup Sauterne
3 eggs

butter and garlic cloves
salt
1 tsp. Worcestershire
½ tsp. mustard
½ tsp. pepper

Mince garlic; cream into butter (or margarine) until of spreading consistency. Remove crusts from bread; spread with garlic butter; place butter side down in shallow baking pan. Beat eggs; add wine, bouillon, seasonings, and cheese. Pour over bread. Bake at 325° for 30 minutes. Serves 4.

HOPPELPOPPEL

4 medium-size potatoes	2 tbls. light cream
1 lb. bacon	1 tsp. salt
3 medium onions, chopped	1 tsp. pepper
(1½ cups)	1 tbls. minced fresh chives
8 eggs	

Cook potatoes in skins in boiling salted water in a large saucepan until barely tender, about 15 minutes. Drain; return to kettle; shake over very low heat to dry. Peel and cut into ¼ inch slices. (Slices should be firm, not overcooked.) Cook the bacon in a large skillet until crisp. Drain on paper, crumble and reserve. Pour off bacon fat from skillet into a cup. Measure and return 5 tablespoons to skillet. Add onion; sauté 5 minutes or until tender. Add potato slices; cook for 10 minutes, turning to brown evenly; add more bacon fat, if needed. Beat eggs in large bowl until foamy; beat in cream, salt, pepper and chives. Sprinkle the reserved bacon over the potatoes. Pour in the egg mixture to cover evenly. Cook over low heat for 8 minutes, shaking the skillet once the eggs begin to set to prevent sticking. Eggs should be well set, but still somewhat moist. Place a warm plate larger than the skillet over the top. Holding both together, turn Hoppelpoppel onto plate (brown side up). Cut into wedges to serve. Serves 8 to 10.

POACHED EGGS MARIE

3 raw potatoes, peeled	⅓ cup grated Gruyère cheese
4 tbls. melted butter or margarine	6 eggs
salt and pepper to taste	heavy sweet cream
dash of freshly ground nutmeg	

Cut potatoes in thin slices; sauté in melted butter over medium heat, stirring frequently, until tender and browned on both sides. Season with salt, pepper, and nutmeg. Spread cooked potatoes on bottom of a shallow, buttered baking dish; sprinkle with the cheese. Break the eggs carefully on top of the cheese, leaving space between the eggs. Salt and pepper to taste. Cover the eggs with cream. Bake at 375° for about 10 minutes or until the eggs are set. Serves 6.

ARTICHOKE RAREBIT

¾ stick butter
1 3-oz. pkg. dried beef
½ cup flour
2 cups light cream
3 cups milk

½ lb. sharp Cheddar, grated
1 can water chestnuts, sliced
1 pkg. frozen artichoke hearts,
    defrosted and cut in pieces
salt and pepper

Melt butter; add dried beef and cook 1 minute. Add flour; stir until smooth; add cream. Add remaining ingredients one at a time. Serve over rice. Serves 10.

CHEESE 'N' FISH IN A CHAFING DISH

2 cups medium white sauce
1 4-oz. can mushrooms, drained,
    or ½ lb. fresh mushrooms
¼ cup butter
1 green pepper, chopped
3 tbls. onion, chopped

1 cup mild Cheddar, grated
1 tsp. salt
dash of pepper
1½ cups frozen asparagus tips, cooked
1 cup canned or cooked fresh
    salmon, flaked

Prepare white sauce in advance. Melt butter in blazer pan of chafing dish. Add mushrooms, green pepper, and onion; cook until tender. Add white sauce, cheese, salt, and pepper. When hot, add salmon and asparagus tips. Serve over chow mein noodles.

Vegetables

ARTICHOKES AND MUSHROOMS

2 pkgs. frozen artichoke hearts
1 lb. small, fresh mushrooms, sliced
¼ cup thinly sliced onion
2 tbls. butter
2 tbls. flour
light cream

dry Vermouth
¼ cup shredded Swiss cheese
½ cup bread crumbs
1 tbls. melted butter
1 tbls. grated Parmesan cheese

Sauté onions in butter until soft; sauté mushrooms until softened but not brown. Cook artichokes in a minimum amount of water just until they can be separated. Drain. Mix onions, mushrooms, and artichokes and spread in a 6-cup casserole. Make a cream sauce by adding flour to melted butter; cook, stirring, until blended. Add equal amounts of cream and Vermouth until of desired thickenss; bring to boil and simmer for 2 minutes. Add grated Swiss cheese; stir until blended. Pour over vegetables. Sprinkle with crumbs mixed with butter and Parmesan. Bake at 350° for 30 minutes. Serves 8.

NEAR EAST STRING BEANS

1 to 1½ lbs. string beans
½ cup tomatoes (fresh or canned)
1 medium onion, chopped

salt and pepper
butter

Wash and cut beans any way desired. Partially cook beans and set aside. Sauté chopped onions in butter until tender. Add drained beans to onions with tomatoes, salt, and pepper and cook until beans are tender. Serves 8 or more.

DRUNKEN BEANS

2 lbs. kidney beans
10 to 12 ozs. fat salt pork
1 cup molasses
2 tbls. brown sugar

1 tsp. dry mustard
½ cup ketchup
2 tsps. salt (optional)
rum

Wash beans in cold water; drain. Cover beans with rum and let soak overnight. Without draining, bring to a simmer; cook until skins burst. (Take a few beans on a spoon, blow on them. Skins will burst if cooked sufficiently.) Drain, reserving liquid. Score salt pork in ½-inch squares, 1-inch deep, being careful not to separate from rind. Place half the beans in a large bean pot; add salt pork; cover with remaining beans. In a saucepan, mix the molasses, brown sugar, mustard, and ketchup. Add 1 cup of reserved rum; bring to boiling point and pour over beans, adding enough rum to cover. Bake at 300° four to six hours or overnight at 250°.

BOURBON BAKED BEANS

2 1-lb. cans baked pea beans
¼ cup Bourbon
2 tbls. brown sugar

1 tbls. dry mustard
1 small can crushed pineapple,
   drained (optional)

Empty beans into casserole dish. Stir in other ingredients. Let stand, covered, at least one hour. Remove cover one hour before serving; bake 1 hour at 375°. Serves 6 to 8.

RED CABBAGE WITH APPLES AND WINE

2-3 lb. head of red cabbage
3-4 tbls. bacon drippings
salt and pepper to taste
1 cup red wine

2 unpeeled tart apples, cored and diced
2 tbls. brown sugar
1 tbls. vinegar

Remove wilted outer leaves of cabbage and core; shred finely; soak for 20 to 30 minutes in cold salted water. Drain well. Sauté the cabbage in bacon drippings, stirring frequently, for several minutes; season to taste with salt and pepper; add wine. Simmer 5 to 6 minutes; add apples. Sprinkle with brown sugar and vinegar; mix well. Cover and simmer 6 to 8 minutes or until cabbage and apples are tender. Serves 4 to 6.

SPANISH CARROTS

3 bunches carrots
2 4-oz. jars pimientoes, drained
6 tbls. butter
1 clove garlic, halved

½ tsp. salt
dash of pepper
2 to 3 tbls. chili sauce

Peel carrots and cook until tender; drain and chop. Coarsely chop the pimientoes. In a saucepan melt butter; add garlic and cook slowly for 3 minutes. Remove garlic and discard. To the butter, add carrots, pimientoes, salt, pepper, and chili sauce. Serve hot. Serves 6 to 8.

SUNSHINE CARROTS

7 or 8 medium carrots
1 tbls. sugar
1 tsp. cornstarch
¼ tsp. salt

¼ tsp. ground ginger
¼ cup orange juice
2 tbls. butter

Carrots may be cooked whole, in chunks, or in slices; cook until tender. Combine remaining ingredients in small saucepan; cook until bubbly, stirring. Let simmer 1 minute; pour over hot carrots; serve immediately. Serves 2 to 4.

CARROT CASSEROLE

6 to 8 cooked carrots
¼ cup carrot cooking liquid
2 tbls. grated onion
2 tbls. horseradish

½ cup mayonnaise
½ tsp. salt
¼ tsp. pepper
stuffing mix; butter; paprika

Cook carrots in enough water to cover; drain; reserve liquid. Cut carrots in bite-size chunks; spread over bottom of a lightly greased shallow casserole. Mix remaining ingredients except stuffing mix. Pour over carrots; toss lightly. Mix enough stuffing with melted butter to spread over top of casserole; sprinkle with paprika. Bake at 325° to 350° for 20 to 30 minutes, or until bubbly. Serves 6.

SWISS CORN PUDDING

36 buttery round crackers
½ tsp. crushed caraway seeds
1 tsp. salt
3 eggs, separated
1 cup milk, scalded
¼ tsp. Tabasco

1½ cups shredded Swiss cheese
1 tbls. melted butter
1 17-oz. can cream-style corn
Bacon curls or sliced olives,
  optional

Crush crackers into fine crumbs; mix with caraway seeds and salt; set aside. Beat egg yolks well; gradually stir in scalded milk and Tabasco. Add crumb mixture, cheese, butter, and corn; combine well. Beat egg whites until stiff, but not dry; fold into corn mixture. Pour into a shallow 6-cup baking dish. Bake in 325° oven for about 40 minutes or until slightly firm to the touch. Garnish with crisp bacon curls or sliced olives. Serves 8.

WEDDING CELEBRATION

The bride is attired in the beautiful heavy creme satin gown Bessie Lincoln wore on her wedding day, April 17, 1900. Sparking cut glass champagne goblets c. 1810, Sevres porcelain c. 1870 and gold plated flatware adorn the festive wedding table.

Wedding Reception

Assorted Tea Sandwiches

Petits Fours

Wedding Cake

Champagne

Mints   Salted Nuts

Wedding cake in photograph courtesy of Mrs. John Burbidge

EGGPLANT CASSEROLE

1 medium-size eggplant
1 tbls. flour
1 tbls. butter
2 medium-size tomatoes, peeled
2 green peppers, chopped
2 medium-size onions, chopped

1 tsp. brown sugar
¼ cup grated cheese
¼ cup bread crumbs
4 slices bacon, crisply crumbled
salt to taste

Peel and dice eggplant. Cook in salted water; drain well. Place eggplant in greased baking dish. Melt butter; blend in flour. Slice tomatoes ½-inch thick. Add to flour mixture; add chopped peppers, onions, sugar, and salt. Cook for 5 minutes. Combine with eggplant in casserole. Mix cheese, bread crumbs, and bacon. Sprinkle over vegetable mixture. Bake at 350° for 35 minutes. Serves 6.

BRAISED BELGIAN ENDIVE

6 medium heads of endive
1 tbls. lemon juice
2 tbls. butter

½ tsp. salt
1 tsp. sugar
1 tbls. beef bouillon granules

Remove and discard any bruised or discolored leaves. Trim stem, being careful not to loosen any leaves; cut a small wedge from center of stem end. Wash endive in cold water; shake off any excess. Melt butter in large skillet; add enough water to just cover the bottom of the pan. Add salt, sugar, and bouillon granules. Bring to boil; add endive in one layer. Reduce heat to a very slow simmer. Cover, cook slowly, turning occasionally, until tender and light brown, about 30 minutes. Add a little water if liquid boils away. If small or medium heads are not available, large ones may be halved. Serves 3 to 6.

FIDDLEHEADS

1 lb. fiddleheads
1 piece lemon peel (optional)

2 tbls. butter, melted
salt and pepper

Fiddleheads are the unrolled fronds of the ostrich fern. To cook, rub off the hairy portions; wash thoroughly and remove the dry, papery scales found in the tightly coiled leaf tips. Trim ends of stalks. Boil in a little water, lightly salted, and with a piece of lemon peel added, for 6 to 8 minutes. Drain. Pour melted butter over the greens. Salt to taste. Serves 4.

KOHLRABI WITH CHEESE

4 kohlrabi
2 tbls. butter or margarine
2 tbls. flour

1 cup milk
¼ cup medium to sharp Cheddar,
  grated

Cut off tops and pare the thickened stems; slice the bulb-like portions of stems. Cook stems and bulbs in boiling salted water about 20 minutes, until barely tender. Drain. If some of the leaves are tender, boil separately; drain. Chop the leaves and add to stems. Melt butter; stir in flour; gradually stir in the milk; cook until thickened. Season to taste. Stir in cheese; cook gently until cheese is melted and combined. Pour over kohlrabi; heat through. Serves 4.

CHEDDAR SQUASH BAKE

2 lbs. yellow summer squash
2 egg yolks, slightly beaten
1 cup dairy sour cream
2 tbls. flour
2 egg whites, stiffly beaten

6 oz. (1½ cups) shredded natural
  Cheddar
4 slices bacon, crisp-cooked and
  crumbled
⅓ cup fine dry bread crumbs
1 tbls. butter or margarine, melted

Scrub squash; trim ends; do not peel. Cook whole, covered, in boiling salted water until tender, about 15 to 20 minutes. Drain; cut into thin slices; sprinkle with salt. (Should give about 6 cups.) Reserve a few nice slices for garnish. Combine egg yolks, sour cream, and flour; fold in the egg whites. Layer in a 12" x 7½" x 2" baking dish half the squash, then half the egg mixture, then half the cheese. Sprinkle with bacon. Repeat the layers. Combine crumbs and butter; sprinkle around edge. Arrange reserved squash on top. Bake at 350° for 20 to 25 minutes. Garnish with bacon curls and parsley if desired. Serves 8 to 10.

LEEKS MIMOSA

2 bunches leeks (about 8)
1 tsp. salt
1 hard-cooked egg

⅓ cup butter or margarine
3 tbls. lemon juice

Trim leeks. Cut off root ends and green stems. Leeks should be about 7 inches long after trimming. Cut each in half lengthwise, being careful not to cut through root end. Wash thoroughly. In a kettle, bring water to boil; add leeks and salt and simmer covered 10 to 15 minutes or just until tender. Drain; chop hard-cooked egg white and yolk separately. Arrange leeks in warm serving dish. Pour melted butter and lemon juice over leeks. Sprinkle egg white and yolk over butter. Serves 6.

MUSHROOMS SUPREME

1 lb. mushrooms; butter
2 beef bouillon cubes
½ cup hot water
¼ cup butter
2 tbls. flour

½ cup cream
1/8 tsp. salt
dash of pepper
½ cup bread crumbs
½ to 1 cup Parmesan cheese

Sauté mushrooms in a little butter. Dissolve bouillon cubes in hot water. Melt ¼ cup of butter; blend in the flour. Add cream, salt and pepper, and bouillon. Turn mushrooms into a buttered casserole; cover with bouillon mixture. Mix bread crumbs and cheese; sprinkle over top of mushroom mixture. Bake at 350° for 30 minutes. Serves 6.

MUSHROOM-BARLEY CASSEROLE

5 cups fresh mushrooms, sliced,
   or 2 cans (6 to 8 oz.) sliced
   mushrooms
1 cup chopped onion
½ cup butter

1½ cups pearl barley
1 4-oz. can pimientoes, chopped
2 cups chicken stock
½ tsp. salt
1/8 tsp. pepper

Preheat oven to 350°. Add barley to mushrooms and onions; sauté in butter until barley is lightly browned. Transfer mixture to large casserole and add remaining ingredients. Cover and bake in 350° oven for 50 to 60 minutes. If barley seems dry during cooking, add more chicken stock (or water). Serves 12.

BAKED ONIONS

10 to 12 large onions, halved
1/8 lb. butter or margarine
1 tbls. dark brown sugar or honey

¼ cup slivered almonds
¼ cup raisins

Place onion halves cut-side up in a greased, shallow casserole. Melt butter; combine with remaining ingredients; pour over onions. Cover. Bake at 350° for 1 hour.

WINE ONIONS

3 tbls. butter
1 10½-oz. can cream of
   mushroom soup
½ cup Sauterne
pepper to taste

2 1-lb. cans whole onions,
   drained
½ cup blanched almonds, toasted
½ cup grated Cheddar

Melt butter in top of double boiler; add soup and wine. Cook, stirring occasionally, about 10 minutes or until mixture is smooth and thick. Season to taste. Add onions and almonds. Turn into greased casserole (1½-quart); sprinkle top with cheese. Bake at 300° to 325° for 20 minutes. Serves 6 to 8.

STUFFED BAKED POTATO FOR DIETERS

1 medium-size Idaho potato
¼ tsp. margarine
1 tsp. chopped onion or chives
1 tbls. low-fat cottage cheese

2 tbls. low-fat yogurt
salt and pepper to taste
1 tsp. paprika
1 tbls. Parmesan cheese

Scrub potato; dry and grease lightly with margarine. Bake at 400° for 40 to 60 minutes or until done. Cut potato in half lengthwise; scoop out pulp, reserving shells. Mash pulp; add onions, cottage cheese, and yogurt. Whip to blend thoroughly. Salt and pepper to taste. (Depending on consistency, a little more yogurt may be added.) Stuff shells with the mixture. Sprinkle paprika and cheese on top. Bake at 350° for 10 minutes. Serves 2.

PARTY POTATOES

8 to 10 peeled potatoes
1 cup sour cream
1 8-oz. pkg. cream cheese

1 tsp. garlic salt
1 tsp. onion salt
Butter and paprika

Boil potatoes until tender; drain; slice. Beat together the sour cream and cream cheese until blended. Add hot potatoes gradually; beat constantly until mixture is light and fluffy. Add seasonings. Spoon into 2-quart casserole; dot with butter; sprinkle with paprika. Refrigerate 24 hours. Bake, covered, at 350° for 45 to 60 minutes. Serves 8 to 10. (Yogurt may be used instead of sour cream.)

SWEET POTATO CASSEROLE

4 or 5 sweet potatoes or yams   ½ tsp. allspice
6 apples, Baldwins or Cortlands   ½ tsp. nutmeg
1½ cups orange juice   3 tbls. butter
½ tsp. salt   ½ cup brown sugar

Parboil potatoes no longer than 20 minutes. Cool; peel; cut in 2-inch chunks. In a well greased casserole, put apples (peeled, cored, and quartered); sweet potato chunks, spices, juice, butter, and brown sugar. Toss lightly. Bake, covered, at 350° for at least ¾ hour. Cool for several hours. Reheat to serve. Serves 6.

SWEET POTATOES WITH APRICOTS

6 large sweet potatoes or yams,   1 tsp. cinnamon
  parboiled   1 cup apricot juice
1 cup brown sugar   1 cup apricot halves, drained
½ tbls. cornstarch   2 tbls. butter
1 tsp. orange rind, grated

Place potatoes in a 1½-quart casserole. Combine brown sugar, cornstarch, orange rind, and cinnamon; add apricot juice. Stir and cook until thickened. Add the apricot halves and the butter. Pour mixture over the potatoes. Bake at 375° for 25 minutes.

SHERRIED SWEET POTATOES

6 large sweet potatoes or yams,   ½ tsp. nutmeg
  cooked and mashed   ¼ cup light cream
2 tbls. butter or margarine   pinch of ginger
2 tbls. brown sugar   ¼ cup medium sherry
½ tsp. cinnamon   salt and pepper to taste

To the mashed potatoes, add all other ingredients. Beat until light and creamy. Salt and pepper to taste. Spoon into a well greased casserole. Bake at 350° for ½ hour. Serves 6 to 8.

PEAS 'N' CAULIFLOWER CASSEROLE

2 16-oz. pkg. frozen cauliflower
1 16-oz. pkg. frozen peas
2 tbls. margarine
2 tbls. flour
1 tsp. curry

1½ cups sour cream
½ cup bread crumbs or finely
   chopped almonds
1 tsp. curry
1 tbls. margarine, melted

Cook the frozen vegetables only until they can be separated; drain; combine. Mix margarine, flour, and 1 teaspoon of curry in a saucepan; heat. Add the sour cream; continue heating. Mix the sauce into vegetables; pour into a 2½-quart casserole. In a skillet, mix the following: ½ cup bread crumbs or almonds, 1 teaspoon curry, and 1 tablespoon margarine. Sprinkle crumb mixture over vegetables and bake at 350° for 35 to 40 minutes. Serves 10 to 12.

SPINACH SOUFFLÉ RING

1½ lbs. spinach, cooked, drained
   and chopped finely OR
2 10½-oz. pkgs. frozen spinach,
   thawed and drained
1 tbls. chopped onion
3 tbls. butter
3 tbls. flour

½ cup milk or beef bouillon
½ cup all-purpose cream
3 eggs, separated
dash of nutmeg
½ cup grated Cheddar
salt and pepper

Sauté onion in butter; add flour, cook, stirring, until smooth. Slowly stir in milk or bouillon, then the cream. When sauce thickens, stir in cheese. Add spinach. Reduce heat and stir in egg yolks which have been lightly beaten. Cook, stirring, for 1 minute; add nutmeg, salt, and pepper. Remove from heat. Beat egg whites until stiff; fold into spinach mixture. Spoon into a greased 7" ring mold. Set in a pan of water and bake at 325° for 30 minutes or until firm. Remove from mold. Serves 8 to 10. (Center may be filled with creamed mushrooms or other vegetable.)

NEW ENGLAND SUCCOTASH

2 16-oz. cans pea beans
   baked in molasses
2 12-oz. cans whole kernel corn

5 slices bacon in ½" pieces
1 large onion, sliced
1 tbls. brown sugar

In a bean pot or 9" x 12" baking dish, layer half each of beans, corn, bacon, and onion; repeat layers. Sprinkle with brown sugar. Bake at 325° for 1½ hours, covered. Remove cover; continue baking about 45 minutes or until onions are light brown. Serves 12.

TOMATOES AU GRATIN

3 tbls. butter
4 large tomatoes, thickly sliced
1 clove garlic, pressed

¼ cup freshly grated Gruyere cheese
¼ cup bread crumbs
salt and pepper

In a lightly buttered baking dish, arrange tomato slices in layers, sprinkling each layer with minced garlic, grated cheese, salt and pepper to taste. Spread bread crumbs over top; dot with butter. Bake at 350° for 15 to 20 minutes until lightly browned on top. Serves 4 to 6.

SOUFFLÉ EN TOMATO

4 medium tomatoes
1 pkg. frozen spinach soufflé, thawed
1 small green pepper, chopped

Dijon-type mustard
grated Cheddar cheese or Parmesan cheese

Cut off tops of tomatoes; scrape out seeds and pulp. Coat inside of tomato shells with mustard. Sprinkle 2 teaspoons of chopped green pepper in each shell. Spoon in thawed soufflé; each tomato should be ⅔ full. Lightly salt and pepper; top with grated cheese. Place on buttered baking dish, and bake 45 minutes at 350°. Garnish with parsley if desired. Serves 4.

CULYANE'S PILAR

2 cups rice
3 cups chicken stock or bouillon
¼ cup margarine
2 tbls. olive oil
2 medium onions, chopped finely
2 tbls. pine nuts

4 tbls. currants
½ tbls. cinnamon
½ tbls. allspice
½ tbls. cumin
1 tbls. salt
1 bunch fresh dill

Combine margarine, olive oil, onions, and pine nuts. Sauté until brown. Add remaining ingredients, except rice. Stir well. When mixture boils, add the rice and stir again. Simmer covered for 20 to 25 minutes. When all the liquid is absorbed, turn off the heat, cover the pan, and let stand 10 minutes. Serve hot. Serves 6.

BALKAN VEGETABLE CASSEROLE (GHIVETCH)

4-oz. beef consommé
2 tbls. olive oil
1½ tsps. tarragon
1½ tsps. summer savory
1 large clove garlic, crushed
½ bay leaf
pepper to taste
2 cups cauliflower flowerets

½ eggplant, cut into ½" pieces
1 cup trimmed brussel sprouts
1 cup sliced carrots
1 cup sliced onions
1 turnip, peeled and cut into ¼" slices
1 green pepper, thinly sliced
1 tomato, cut into pieces

In small saucepan, combine first 7 ingredients; cook the mixture over moderate heat for 5 minutes. In a shallow heavy baking dish, combine all the vegetables and stir to mix. Pour the sauce over the vegetables. Cover and bake about 45 minutes at 350° or until vegetables are as tender as you prefer. If put together ahead and chilled, increase baking time to at least one hour. Serves 8 to 10.

Desserts

WEDDING FRUIT CAKE

1 cup shortening	3 cups raisins
1½ cups brown sugar	2 cups chopped dates
6 eggs separated	1 cup currants
¼ cup fruit juice	½ cup citron, chopped
(orange or pineapple)	1 cup candied orange, chopped
¾ tsp. baking soda	2 cups nuts
½ cup molasses	2 cups sifted flour
1 10-oz. jar maraschino cherries	¼ tsp. nutmeg
½ cup finely cut candied	¼ tsp. cloves
pineapple	½ tsp.cinnamon

Cream shortening and brown sugar until fluffy. Add beaten egg yolks and fruit juice. Dissolve baking soda in heated molasses and add to shortening mixture. Combine all the fruit in a large bowl and sprinkle all the flour over the fruit, mixing thoroughly with a large spoon or rubber spatula until all the fruit is coated with flour. Add nuts. Combine both mixtures and fold in stiffly beaten egg whites and spices. Line the bottoms and sides of two 8½" x 4½" x 2½" loaf pans with brown paper, allowing ½" to extend above on all sides. Pour batter into pans, filling ⅔ full. Bake at 275° for 2½ hours until done. Cool in pans.

FROSTING

1 cup milk	1 cup butter or margarine
2 tbls. flour	1 tsp. vanilla
1 cup sugar	

Combine and cook milk and flour, stirring constantly over low heat until smooth; do not allow milk to boil. Remove from heat; cover with waxed paper; let cool. Cream together the sugar and butter; add vanilla. Add cooled milk mixture to creamed sugar. Beat 10 minutes with electric mixer, scraping down sides of bowl with spatula to combine all ingredients.

ZIA'S FRUIT CAKE

½ cup butter or margarine
1 cup sugar
3 eggs, beaten
1 cup flour
½ tsp. baking powder
¼ tsp. salt
½ tsp. nutmeg

¼ cup milk
¼ cup molasses
¼ tsp. baking soda
1½ lbs. seedless raisins
½ lb. mixed candied fruit
2 cups chopped pecans
¼ cup bourbon or brandy

Cream butter with sugar, add eggs. Mix flour, baking powder, salt and nutmeg and add to butter mixture. Add milk. Put soda in molasses and mix; add to above. Add raisins, nuts, fruit, and liquor. Pour into well-greased and floured pans (1 large or 2 small loaves). Bake 2 hours at 300°. Wrapped in foil, will keep indefinitely.

MARY TODD'S WHITE CAKE

1 cup butter
2 cups sugar
3 cups sifted cake flour
1 cup milk

1 cup finely chopped blanched almonds
3 tsps. baking powder
whites of 6 eggs
1 tsp. vanilla

Cream butter and sugar. Sift flour and baking powder together three times; add to butter and sugar, alternating with the milk. Stir in nut meats and beat well. Fold in the stiffly beaten egg whites and the flavoring. Pour into 2 greased and floured 9″ layer pans. Bake at 350° for 30 to 35 minutes. Let set 10 minutes, then turn out onto wire racks and cool before frosting.

CHOCOLATE CAKE

2 cups sugar
½ cup shortening
½ stick butter
2 cups sifted flour
⅔ cup cocoa
1½ tsps. soda

¾ tsp. salt
1¼ cups milk
¾ tsp. baking powder
4 eggs
1 tsp. vanilla

Beat together sugar, shortening, and butter until light and fluffy. Sift together flour, cocoa, soda, and salt; add to butter-sugar mixture with ¾ cup milk; beat at medium speed 1½ minutes. Add baking powder; beat ½ minute. Add eggs, ½ cup milk, and vanilla. Beat 1 more minute until well mixed. Flour and paper two 9″ round pans. Bake 35 minutes in a 350° oven. Let cool 10 minutes, then remove from pans and cool on racks. Split layers and spread with apricot butter and then ice.

APRICOT BUTTER

1 11-oz. pkg. dried apricots
½ cup sugar

water

Place apricots in pan and cover with water; add sugar. Cook slowly until tender, about 15 minutes. Blend well in blender. Use as needed.

ICING

1 6-oz. pkg. chocolate chips

¼ lb. butter or margarine

Melt together slowly; mix and spread over sides and top of cake.

PINEAPPLE PUDDING CAKE

2 16-oz. cans crushed pineapple,
   drained
1 pint heavy cream
1 pkg. instant vanilla pudding

1 tsp. vanilla
2 pkgs. ladyfingers
maraschino cherries

Whip heavy cream in large bowl till stiff, add vanilla, and blend. Make instant pudding in large bowl according to manufacturer's directions. Add drained pineapple to pudding mixture and fold in. Fold in whipped cream. Put ⅓ of mixture in glass dish. Separate 1 package of ladyfingers and place on top of mixture. Repeat procedure, alternating whipped cream and ladyfingers, ending with whipped cream mixture on top. Decorate with cherries.

PISTACHIO CAKE

1 box yellow butter cake mix
4 eggs
¾ cup oil
½ pint sour cream

1 3-oz. box pistachio instant
   pudding mix
½ cup chopped pecans

FROSTING

1 pint whipping cream
1 3-oz. pkg. pistachio instant
   pudding

4 drops green food coloring

Combine first 5 ingredients; add pecans; batter will be thick. Pour into greased bundt pan or 11″ angel cake pan. Bake 1 hour at 350°. Remove and frost when cool. Frosting: combine all ingredients and whip until stiff.

WHEAT GERM CARROT CAKE

1½ cups cooking oil
2 cups packed brown sugar
4 eggs
1 tbls. grated orange peel
1½ tsps. vanilla
3 cups grated carrots
1½ cups vacuum-packed wheat
   germ

2 cups flour
3 tsps. baking powder
1½ tsps. salt
1½ tsps. cinnamon
¾ tsp. nutmeg
1 cup raisins
¾ cup chopped pecans

Beat together oil, sugar, eggs. Mix in orange peel, vanilla, carrots. Combine wheat germ, flour, baking powder, salt, cinnamon, nutmeg. Stir into carrot mixture. Add raisins and pecans. Turn into greased and floured 10″ bundt pan. Bake at 350° for 60 to 70 minutes, or until toothpick comes out clean. Cool in pan 10 minutes; remove from pan to rack to cool. Serve with whipped cream or whipped cream cheese.

DOCTOR BIRD CAKE
The Doctor Bird is found only in Jamaica

3 cups sifted flour
1 tsp. cinnamon
1 tsp. salt
1 tsp. baking soda
1½ cups sugar

1 8-oz. can crushed pineapple and juice
1½ tsps. vanilla
2 cups diced bananas (4 ripe ones)
1½ cups cooking oil
3 eggs

Measure dry ingredients and sift together. Dice bananas; measure and add to dry ingredients along with vanilla, eggs, and crushed pineapple and juice. Stir to blend. DO NOT BEAT. Pour into 10-inch tube pan. Bake at 350° for 1 hour. Glaze with mixture of 1 tablespoon of rum and ¾ cup of confectioner's sugar.

CANDY CAKE

1 cup (2 sticks) sweet butter
2 cups sugar
4 eggs
½ cup buttermilk*
1 tsp. baking soda
3½ cups all-purpose flour
1 8-oz. box chopped dates

1 cup coarsely chopped walnuts
1 cup finely chopped walnuts
1 4-oz. pkg. sweetened shredded
   coconut
1 lb. orange candy slices, diced
½ cup orange juice
1½ cups confectioner's sugar

Cream butter and 2 cups sugar until smooth. Add the eggs one at a time, and beat well after each addition. Dissolve baking soda in buttermilk and add to creamed mixture. Place flour in a large bowl and add dates, nuts, coconut, and candy. Stir well. Add the floured mixture to the creamed mixture. This makes a very stiff dough that should be mixed with the hands. Pour into a greased 9″ x 13″ rectangular cake pan or tube pan. Bake in preheated 250° oven for 2½ to 3 hours. Test for doneness with a toothpick which should come out clean. When the cake has almost completed baking, combine and warm over low heat the orange juice and sugar. Pour over the cake as soon as it is taken from the oven. Let the cake stand in the pan, covered with plastic wrap or foil, overnight in the refrigerator.
*Or substitute: ½ cup milk combined with 1½ tsp. vinegar.

GUM-DROP CAKE

½ cup butter
1 cup sugar
2 eggs, beaten slightly
½ cup milk
1½ cups flour
2 tsps. baking powder

1 tsp. almond extract
1 tsp. vanilla
1 cup sultana raisins (optional)
1 lb. gum drops (no black ones)
¼ tsp. salt

Cream butter; add sugar; add beaten eggs. Chop raisins if used; slice large gum drops, halve small ones; toss gum drops in a little flour. Mix together and sift the remaining flour, baking powder, and salt 3 times. Add alternately with the milk to the egg mixture; add raisins and gum drops; add the almond and vanilla extracts. Spoon into a lightly greased and floured 9″ angel cake pan. Bake at 350° for 40 minutes. Cool, inverted, on wire rack.

PUMPKIN CAKE ROLL

3 large eggs
1 cup sugar
⅔ cup cooked pumpkin
1 tsp. lemon juice
¾ cup flour
1 tsp. baking powder

2 tsps. cinnamon
1 tsp. ginger
½ tsp. nutmeg
½ tsp. salt
1 cup finely chopped walnuts

Beat eggs on high speed for 5 minutes. Gradually beat in sugar. Stir in pumpkin and lemon juice. Stir together flour, baking powder, cinnamon, ginger, nutmeg, and salt. Fold into batter. Line a greased 15″ x 10″ x 1″ pan with waxed paper and grease the paper. Spread batter evenly in pan. Sprinkle with walnuts. Bake in 375° oven for 12 to 15 minutes until cake tests done when toothpick is inserted. Turn out onto towel that has been sprinkled with confectioner's sugar. Remove paper; starting at narrow end roll up towel and cake together. Cool for 2 hours. Unroll. Spread with filling and roll up again. Serves 10 to 12.

CREAM CHEESE FILLING

1 cup confectioner's sugar
6 oz. cream cheese

4 tbls. butter
½ tsp. vanilla

Whip sugar with cheese, butter and vanilla. Spread over cake. Roll up. Chill until served.

DARK APPLE CAKE

4 cups sliced or chopped apples
1½ cups sugar
2 eggs
½ cup oil
2 cups flour
2 tsps. baking soda

2 tsps. cinnamon
1 tsp. salt
½ tsp. nutmeg
2 tsps. vanilla
1 cup raisins or chopped dates
1 cup chopped nuts, optional

Chop apples and add sugar. Let stand 30 minutes. Using an electric mixer and another bowl, mix remaining ingredients, except raisins. Mixture will be crumbly. Add apples, raisins, and nuts. Blend together with large spoon. Pour into greased and sugared bundt pan. It is better to grease and sugar the pan instead of flouring it. Bake at 350° for 45 to 50 minutes. Serves 10 to 12.

HUMMINGBIRD CAKE

3 cups flour
1½ cups sugar
1½ tsps. vanilla
1½ cups oil
2 cups mashed bananas
    (8-10 small)

3 eggs
1 tsp. baking soda
1 tsp. salt
½ cup nuts
1 8-oz. can crushed pineapple,
    undrained

Mix all by hand. Bake in greased, floured tube, bundt pan, or 11″ angel cake pan. Bake at 300° for 1½ hours to 1¾ hours until slight cracks show on top. Cool 1 hour before removing from pan.

ICING

8 ozs. softened cream cheese
¼ lb. butter

1 lb. confectioner's sugar
1 tsp. vanilla

Cream together the cream cheese and butter. Add the sugar and vanilla. Blend well.

CHRISTMAS DINNER

At the historic Ropes mansion, Salem, a festive holiday table set with a dinner service of Chinese export porcelain, Nanking pattern c. 1817. The Irish glassware c. 1817 is from a complete 182 piece service of matching tumblers, wine glasses, and decanters.

The following quotation from a letter written to Nathaniel Ropes IV by his sister Sally Ropes Orne describes a Christmas dinner party that she gave for six friends in 1848.

"It is the present fashion (of course evanescent, as all fashions are) to have the dinner kept in the kitchen till the guests are seated. On my table was a pint decanter of Maderia wine and another of Sherry, also a bottle of Hock wine (expensive, one dollar and twenty five cents, but not so palatable as good cider, tasting much like it) I first invited them to partake of these liquors, then signified by a nod to the waiter that I was ready, when a Tureen of Oyster soup made its apperance- on its removal a pair of handsome boiled chickens, weight eleven pounds, and a good sized ham were substituted with suitable accompainments, caper sauce, mashed potatoes with butter and milk mixed with it, and squash. This course displaced, came a noble turkey, pan gravy and liver sauce, cranberry ditto, mashed potato browned on top and marked off in diamonds, with sweet or Carolina ditto: the upper cloth was then taken away, when a plum pudding and hard sauce were placed on the table, afterwards mince pies and cream pudding. Then the things were all carried out, the white cloth being removed and on the green fruit cloth were displayed, in the center a plated basket of Baldwin apples, at top a large glass dish of grapes, at the other end a glass dish corresponding in use to the one just named, and side dishes containing square wall nuts and raisens, with a quart decanter of Sherry wine planted by the gentlemen. Every article was charmingly cooked and the day, I assure you, went off finely."

Letter courtesy of the Trustees of the Ropes Memorial, Salem.

BLUEBERRY GINGERBREAD

½ cup cooking oil (or shortening)　1 tsp. cinnamon
1 cup sugar　½ tsp. nutmeg
½ tsp. salt　1 tsp. baking soda
3 tbls. molasses　1 cup fresh or frozen blueberries
1 egg　1 cup buttermilk (or sour milk)
2 cups all-purpose flour　2 tbls. sugar
½ tsp. ginger

With electric mixer, beat together oil, sugar, salt, and molasses. Beat in egg.
Combine flour, spices, and baking soda; dredge blueberries with 2 tablespoons
of flour mixture. Add remaining flour mixture to first mixture, alternating with
buttermilk, beating after each addition. Stir in blueberries. Pour into greased
and floured 15 x 7½-inch baking dish. Sprinkle top with remaining sugar. Bake
in 350° oven 35 to 40 minutes, or until toothpick inserted into gingerbread will
come out clean. Cut into squares. Serve warm with butter, or with whipped
cream for dessert. Makes 12 squares.

VIENNESE TORTE

1 6-oz. pkg. chocolate bits　2 tbls. sifted confectioner's sugar
½ cup butter or margarine　1 tsp. vanilla
¼ cup water　1 12-oz. loaf pound cake
4 slightly beaten egg yolks

In heavy saucepan heat chocolate, butter, and water over low heat, stirring until blended. Cool slightly and add egg yolks, sugar, and vanilla. Stir until
smooth. Chill until it is of spreading consistency, about 45 minutes. Slice cake
horizontally in six layers. Spread chocolate mixture between layers. Frost top
and sides. Chill at least 40 to 60 minutes or overnight. If overnight, cover lightly
with foil. Serves 8 to 10.

WEARY WILLIE CAKE

1 cup flour
1 cup sugar
2 tsps. baking powder
½ tsp. salt
2 squares chocolate, melted

¼ cup butter, melted
1 egg
milk
1 tsp. vanilla
confectioner's sugar

Sift together the flour, sugar, baking powder, and salt. Mix melted chocolate and melted butter. Break egg into measuring cup; fill with enough milk to make 1 cup. Add chocolate and egg mixtures to flour mixture; beat together for about 2 minutes. Add vanilla. Pour into small angel cake tin. Bake at 350° for about 35 mintues or until an inserted cake tester tests clean. Remove from pan. Place a paper-lace doily over top; sprinkle with confectioner's sugar. Remove doily.

PRUNE CAKE

1½ cups sugar
1 cup cooking oil
3 eggs
1 tbls. cinnamon
1 tbls. allspice
1 tbls. nutmeg
½ tsp. salt

2 tsps. vanilla
2 cups flour
1 tsp. baking soda
1 cup sour cream
1½ cups chopped prunes
1 cup chopped nuts

Combine sugar and oil; add eggs, one at a time, beating well after each addition. Add spices, salt, and vanilla. Combine flour and soda and add to egg mixture alternately with sour cream. Add chopped prunes and nuts. Pour into greased and floured bundt pan. Bake at 350° for 50 to 60 minutes or until cake tester comes out clean.

TOMATO SOUP CAKE

2 cups flour	½ cup oil
1 cup sugar	2 eggs
1 tsp. baking soda	1 cup raisins
2 tsps. baking powder	1 cup chopped nuts
1 tsp. cinnamon	1 3-oz. pkg. cream cheese
1 tsp. nutmeg	2 cups confectioner's sugar
½ tsp. ground cloves	1 tsp. vanilla
1 10¾-oz. can tomato soup	1 tbls. milk

Sift together the flour, 1 cup sugar, baking soda, baking powder, cinnamon, nutmeg, and cloves. Add soup, oil and eggs. Beat well, at least 1 minute with mixer. Add raisins and nuts. Pour into greased tube or loaf (10" x 5" x 3") pan. Bake at 350° for 1 hour.

FROSTING

Mix cream cheese, confectioner's sugar, vanilla, and milk together; spread on cooled cake.

ORANGES GEORGE V

4 cups fresh orange segments	slivered peel of 1½ oranges
1¼ cups sugar	½ tsp. vanilla
1¼ cups boiling water	1½ tsps. gelatin
⅔ cup orange juice	1 tbls. water

Soften gelatin in 1 tablespoon of water. Place all other ingredients except orange segments in saucepan; boil 5 to 10 minutes until syrup is thick and slivered peel translucent. Remove from heat; add gelatin; allow to cool slightly. Add orange segments. Chill overnight. Serves 6 to 8.

RHUBARB DELIGHT

2 large juice oranges	2 navel oranges
water	4 cups rhubarb
1½ cups sugar	2 tbls. liqueur - Cointreau,
pinch of salt	Triple Sec, or Grand Marnier

Squeeze juice from the 2 large juice oranges; add juice to enough water to make 2 cups. Add sugar and salt. Cook in saucepan until slightly thickened. Cut peel from oranges into thin strips, removing all white membrane. Cook in boiling water 5 minutes; drain. Put 4 cups rhubarb, sliced ½-inch thick, in a deep (3-quart) casserole; pour orange syrup over rhubarb; add cooked peel. Bake, covered, at 325° for 15 minutes, or until rhubarb is just tender. Remove from oven; uncover. Peel 2 naval oranges; remove all membrane; slice crosswise. Cut slices into quarters; add to rhubarb. Add 2 tablespoons liqueur. Cool and chill. Serves 6 to 8.

BURGUNDY PEARS

4 firm, ripe Bartlett pears	½ cup currant jelly
½ cup sugar	¼ tsp. red food coloring
⅔ cup water	½ cup Burgundy wine

Heat together until dissolved the sugar, water, and jelly; add the red food coloring. Peel and core whole pears leaving stems attached. Place pears in syrup and simmer gently until pears are tender, basting frequently to tint pears and coat with syrup. Remove from heat; add wine to syrup; cool in refrigerator. To serve, place pears in individual dishes; divide syrup evenly, spooning over the pears. Serve with whipped or sour cream; sprinkle very lightly with cinnamon.

LEMON FLUFF

4 eggs, separated	2 tbls. gelatin
1 lemon — rind and juice	½ pt. whipping cream
¾ cup sugar	ladyfingers or pie crust
2 tbls. water	

Mix sugar, rind (grated) and juice of lemon, and egg yolks in top of double boiler. Bring to boiling point, stirring. Dissolve gelatin in water; add to lemon mixture. Beat egg whites until stiff; fold into lemon-gelatin mixture. Surround a glass serving dish with split ladyfingers; carefully pour in the lemon mixture. Chill. When ready to serve, top with whipped cream. **OR** pour into baked pie shell. Regrigerate over night. Serves 6 to 8. (Optional: sprinkle ladyfingers with white creme de menthe.)

FROZEN LEMON MOUSSE

3 egg yolks
¼ cup lemon juice
grated rind of lemon
1/8 tsp. salt

1 cup sugar
3 egg whites, beaten stiffly
1 cup whipped cream
vanilla wafer crumbs

Beat egg yolks well. Combine with lemon juice and rind, salt, and sugar in saucepan. Cook for seven minutes, stirring constantly. Mixture should coat spoon. Cool. Fold in 1 cup whipped cream and 3 whipped egg whites. Sprinkle light layer of crumbs over bottom of ice cube tray. Spoon lemon mixture over crumbs. Sprinkle more crumbs over top. Freeze. Serves 6.

ANGEL'S DELIGHT

1 3-oz. pkg. lemon gelatin
12 large marshmallows, quartered
4 coconut cakes, crumbled
2 cups water, heated

½ cup maraschino cherries, coarsely
  chopped
1 8-oz. can crushed pineapple
1 pt. whipping cream, whipped

Drain pineapple; add enough water to juice to make 2 cups of liquid. Dissolve gelatin in heated liquid. Let cool and thicken slightly. Whip until light and fluffy. Add marshmallows, crumbled coconut cakes, crushed pineapple, and chopped cherries. Fold in whipped cream. Refrigerate overnight. Serves 12.

APRICOT TORTONI

1⅓ cups vanilla wafer crumbs
1 tsp. almond extract
3 tbls. melted butter
3 pts. vanilla ice cream, softened

1 12-oz. jar apricot preserves
⅓ cup toasted chopped almonds
  (optional)

Mix crumbs with almond extract and butter. Add toasted almonds if desired. Press ⅓ of the crumb mixture into bottom of a 9"-square pan. Add a layer of ice cream; drizzle half the preserves over top. Repeat layers. Top with last ⅓ of crumbs. Freeze several hours until firm. Serve with dollop of whipped cream. Serves 9 to 12.

TORTA di RICOTTA

2 lbs. Ricotta cheese
1⅔ cups sugar
1 tsp. vanilla extract
¼ cup white or chocolate crème
   de cacoa

¼ cup semi-sweet chocolate bits
¼ cup candied fruits and peels, diced
2 doz. ladyfingers
whole candied cherries

Combine first 4 ingredients in large mixing bowl. Beat 10 minutes until fluffy. Stir in chocolate and citrus bits. Line sides and bottom of a glass bowl with split halves of ladyfingers, rounded sides out. Pour half of mixture into bowl. Add another layer of ladyfingers and top with remainder of the mix. Garnish with candied cherries and/or chocolate curls. Refrigerate, covered with plastic wrap, overnight. Serves 8 to 12.

COFFEE MARSHMALLOW PUDDING

1 lb. marshmallows
2 cups strong boiling coffee
1¼ cups cream, whipped

1 or 2 tbls. brandy or rum, to taste
¼ cup chopped pecans
bitter chocolate; cherries

Melt marshmallows in boiling coffee; let cool, but not harden. Fold in one cup of whipped cream, brandy or rum, and nuts. Pour into molds or individual serving dishes. Before serving, garnish with a dollop of whipped cream, shaved chocolate, and a maraschino cherry for color.

SWEDISH CRÈME

1 pt. whipping cream
½ cup sugar
1 envelope gelatin

2 tbls. cold water
1 pt. sour cream
dash of salt

Heat cream until tiny bubbles form at edge of pan. Add sugar, salt, and the gelatin which has been softened in the cold water. Mix well. Add sour cream, mixing with whisk until well blended and smooth. Pour into a bowl or individual parfait glasses. Refrigerate for several hours. Serve with crushed strawberries, raspberries, or mandarin oranges. Serves 6 to 8.

EMPEROR'S CHOICE

1¾ cups graham cracker crumbs
¼ cup chopped walnuts
¼ lb. margarine, softened
½ tsp. cinnamon
3 eggs
1 cup sugar

2 tsps. vanilla
½ tsp. almond extract
2 8-oz. pkgs. cream cheese, softened
3 cups sour cream
2 cans blueberry or cherry pie filling
or 1 box (16-oz.) frozen strawberries

Mix cracker crumbs, nuts, margarine, and cinnamon together; press on bottom and sides of a spring-form pan. Beat eggs; add sugar, vanilla, almond extract, and cream cheese, blending thoroughly. Add sour cream; beat again. Pour mixture into crust and bake at 375° for 40 minutes. Let cool in refrigerator 4 hours or overnight. Cover with pie filling. **OR,** thaw and strain berries; add 2 tablespoons of cornstarch to juice and boil until thickened and clear. Add strawberries. When cool, pour over cheese cake. Refrigerate 2 hours before serving. Serves 8 to 10.

CHERRY SURPRISE

3 egg whites
½ tsp. cream of tartar
1 cup sugar
1 tsp. vanilla

1 cup soda crackers, broken into
    small pieces
½ cup chopped walnuts
1 large pkg. topping mix, whipped
2 cans cherry pie filling

Beat egg whites and cream of tartar until stiff. Add sugar and vanilla. Fold in crackers and nuts. Spread in heavily greased pan, 13″ x 9″. Bake at 350° for 20 minutes or until evenly browned. Cool. Spread with layer of whipped topping, then pie filling. Chill. Can be made day before serving. Serves 12.

FROSTY STRAWBERRY SQUARES

1 cup sifted all-purpose flour
1¼ cups brown sugar
½ cup chopped California walnuts
½ cup butter or margarine, melted
2 egg whites

1 cup white sugar
2 cups sliced fresh strawberries*
2 tbls. lemon juice
1 cup heavy cream whipped

Stir together the flour, brown sugar, walnuts, and butter. Spread evenly in a shallow baking pan. Bake in 350° oven, stirring occasionally, for 20 minutes. Combine egg whites, sugar, berries, and lemon juice in a large bowl. With an electric beater at high speed, whip until stiff peaks form (about 10 minutes). Fold in whipped cream. Sprinkle ⅔ of crumb mixture in a 13″ x 9″ x 2″ baking dish. Spoon strawberry mixture over crumbs. Top with remaining crumbs. Freeze 6 hours or overnight. Cut into 10 or 12 squares. Decorate squares with whole berries.
*Or use one 10-ounce package of sliced frozen berries partially thawed. Reduce white sugar to ⅔ cup.

CRANBERRY REFRIGERATOR DESSERT

2 cups (½ lb.) fresh cranberries
1 cup diced banana
½ cup sugar
2 cups vanilla wafer crumbs
6 tbls. butter, melted

½ cup butter
1 cup sugar
2 eggs
½ cup chopped nuts
1 cup whipping cream

Grind 2 cups of fresh cranberries; combine with diced banana and ½ cup sugar; set aside. Combine 2 cups vanilla wafer crumbs and 6 tablespoons of melted butter. Press ½ crumb mixture in bottom of 9″ x 9″ pan. Cream ½ cup butter with 1 cup sugar until light. Add 2 eggs and beat until fluffy. Fold in ½ cup chopped nuts. Spread over crumb layer. Top with cranberry mixture. Whip 1 cup whipping cream just until soft peaks form. Spread over all. Sprinkle with remaining crumbs. Chill 6 hours or freeze. Serves 12.

PINA COLADA MOLD

1¾ cup canned unsweetened
   pineapple juice
1 envelope plain gelatin
¼ cup white rum

¼ cup sweetened canned cream of
   coconut (room temperature)
1 10-oz. pkg. frozen sweetened
   strawberries, thawed

Sprinkle gelatin over ½ cup pineapple to soften; bring remaining juice to a boil and pour over gelatin mixture, stirring until dissolved. Add rum and cream of coconut, stirring until well blended. Pour into 6-cup ring mold or 6 individual molds. Serve with defrosted strawberries. Serves 6.

ANGEL'S DESSERT

5 egg whites	1 pt. heavy cream
¼ tsp. salt	1 tbls. sugar
½ tsp. cream of tartar	1 tsp. vanilla
1½ cups sugar	1 box frozen strawberries or peaches

Beat egg whites and salt until foamy; add cream of tartar; continue beating until eggs stand in peaks. Add sugar and vanilla slowly. Place in greased 9" pie plate or 12" x 7½" x 2" pan. Preheat oven to 450°. Put pan into oven; close oven; turn off heat. Leave in oven overnight. **Do not open** oven door after putting meringue in. Top with whipped cream flavored with vanilla and one tablespoon of sugar. Refrigerate 6 hours. Cut into wedges or squares; top with defrosted fruit just before serving.

FOOLPROOF CHOCOLATE MOUSSE

1 6-oz. pkg. chocolate bits	¾ cup hot coffee
4 egg yolks	4 egg whites
2 tbls. apricot brandy	3 tbls. sugar

Combine chocolate and coffee in blender; mix at high speed for 30 seconds or until smooth. Add egg yolks and brandy; mix at high speed for 30 seconds. Beat egg whites until foamy and doubled in volume; gradually beat in sugar; continue beating until whites hold soft peaks. Fold in chocolate mixture; continue until no white streaks remain. Spoon into individual bowls or sherbert glasses. Chill at least 1 hour. Serves 6.

CHOCOLATE MOUSSE

18 ozs. semisweet chocolate	¼ cup sherry
¾ cup water	9 eggs
¼ cup butter	

Separate whites and yolks of eggs. Put the chocolate and water into top of a double boiler; stir until chocolate is thick and creamy. Remove from heat. Add butter and stir. Add sherry and stir. Stir the yolks together so that they are broken. Stir into chocolate mix, pouring slowly and stirring constantly. Beat the egg whites until they form a soft peak and fold very carefully into the chocolate. Pour mixture into mousse glasses and chill. Makes about 18 (4 oz.) servings.

CHESTNUT SOUFFLÉ GRAND MARNIER

4 whole eggs	¼ cup (2 ozs.) Grand Marnier
6 egg yolks	2 tbls. gelatin, dissolved in a little water
¾ cup sugar	½ pt. heavy cream, whipped
1¼ lbs. chestnuts	ladyfingers

In mixer, whip whole eggs, yolks, and sugar to a stiff peak. In a blender, reduce chestnuts to fine crumbs; mix with Grand Marnier. Reduce speed of mixer and add chestnuts to egg mixture. Add dissolved gelatin; mix for 1 minute. Fold in the whipped cream. Turn into a 1½-quart mold or souffle dish. Refrigerate approximately 4 hours. Unmold; garnish sides with ladyfingers. Serves 10.

IRISH COFFEE MOUSSE

2 envelopes plus 1 tsp. plain gelatin	⅓ cup Irish whiskey
3⅔ cups cold black coffee	1 tbls. grated orange rind
½ cup sugar	1 cup heavy cream, whipped

In small saucepan, sprinkle gelatin over ⅔ cup of coffee; let stand 5 minutes. Add sugar; stir over low heat until sugar dissolves. Add rest of coffee. Stir in whiskey and orange rind. Refrigerate, stirring occasionally, until slightly thickened. Put 2 cups of mixture in a bowl; fold in the whipped cream. Spoon into slightly oiled 6-cup mold and refrigerate until nearly set. Keep remaining coffee mixture at room temperature. When mold is almost set, add the remaining mixture to the top of it. Chill mold until set. Serves 6.

To unmold: run a knife around edge to loosen the gelatin. Tilt mold toward you; at same time insert knife to bottom of mold, gently pulling gelatin away from side of mold to break air lock; remove knife. Place a plate over mold; holding together firmly, turn over so that plate is on bottom. Gently shake sideways once or twice. If gelatin doesn't slide out, turn over and repeat process. Dipping this mold in warm water will produce a "melted" look.

BLUEBERRY SLUMP

6 slices white bread
  (firm quality)
1 pt. (3 cups) blueberries

½ cup sugar
½ cup water
cinnamon

Trim crusts from bread; lightly butter both sides and sprinkle very lightly with cinnamon. Bring berries, sugar, and water to a slow boil and cook, stirring occasionally, for 10 minutes. Cool. Arrange berries and bread alternately in glass loaf pan. Chill in refrigerator several hours or overnight. Turn out of pan and slice. Serve with whipped cream or vanilla ice cream. (May also be served warm.) Serves 6 to 8.

COCONUT ICE CREAM PIE

2 tbls. butter
1 7-oz. pkg. shredded coconut
whipping cream

coffee ice cream
chocolate shot ("jimmies")

Use butter to generously grease a 9″ pie plate. Press coconut over bottom and sides of a pie plate to form a shell. Bake 10 to 12 minutes at 350°. Remove from oven; when cool, fill with coffee ice cream. Top with whipped cream; sprinkle with chocolate shot. Serves 6 to 8.

APPLE TORTE

½ cup butter or margarine
⅔ plus ¼ cup sugar
1½ tsps. vanilla
1 cup flour
1 8-oz. pkg. cream cheese
  at room temperature

1 egg
4 cups apples, peeled and sliced
½ tsp. cinnamon
¼ cup almonds, slivered

Cream together ½ cup butter, ⅓ cup sugar, and 1 tsp. vanilla. Blend in 1 cup flour. Spread mixture on bottom and sides of 9″ spring-form pan. Combine the cream cheese, ¼ cup sugar, egg, and ½ tsp. vanilla. Pour into pan. Toss apples with ⅓ cup sugar and cinnamon. Put on top of cream cheese layer; sprinkle with almonds. Bake at 450° for 10 minutes; lower to 375° for 25 minutes longer. Serves 6 to 8.

CHOCOLATE "INDIAN" PUDDING

3 cups cornflakes
2 cups milk, heated
4 tsps. cocoa
½ cup sugar

2 tsps. butter
1 egg, beaten
dash of salt

Pour heated milk over cornflakes in 1½-quart casserole. Mix together the cocoa and sugar; add to casserole. Add remaining ingredients; mix gently. Bake at 300° for 1 hour. Serve with whipped cream. Serves 4.

APPLE MACAROON

6 medium apples; peeled, cored,
  and sliced
1 cup sugar
1 cup flour

1 to 2 tbls. cinnamon
¼ lb. butter or margarine
1 egg, slightly beaten

Spread apples in greased pie plate. Mix sugar, flour, and cinnamon; add egg. Melt butter and add to form a paste-like mixture. Spread over apples. Bake at 325° for 40 to 50 minutes. Serves 6 to 8.

EMERGENCY PUDDING

4 to 5 slices of dark bread
½ cup molasses
¼ tsp. ginger

½ tsp. cinnamon
milk

Butter the bread and break into small pieces. Put in buttered dish; add molasses, ginger, and cinnamon; cover well with milk. Bake in slow oven until it is consistency of Indian Pudding. Serve with cream or ice cream. Serves 6.

BANGOR PUDDING & CREAM SAUCE

1⅓ cups cracker crumbs
1 cup boiling water
1 pt. milk
¼ tsp. salt
⅓ cup molasses
1 egg, slightly beaten
½ lb. seedless raisins, cut in halves

Cream Sauce
1⅓ cups heavy cream
1 cup sifted powdered sugar
1 egg white, stiffly beaten
1½ tsps. vanilla
1 egg yolk

Moisten the cracker crumbs with the boiling water and let stand until cool. Add milk, molasses, salt, egg, and raisins; turn into a 4-cup buttered mold. Steam in crockpot for 8 hours. Remove cover when done and set aside to cool (2 hours). Cream Sauce: Beat cream until stiff; add powdered sugar, egg white, vanilla, and lastly yolk that has been beaten with a spoon. Serve over Bangor Pudding. Serves 8.

INDIAN PUDDING

5 cups milk
¼ cup corn meal
⅔ cup light molasses

1 tsp. salt
1 tsp. ginger
1 tbls. butter

Scald 4 cups of milk in double boiler; add corn meal and cook 20 minutes. Add molasses, salt, ginger, and butter. Put into 1 quart ovenproof casserole. Pour 1 cup of milk over mixture. Bake in slow oven (300° to 325°) for 3 hours. Serve warm.

CHOCOLATE WAFFLES

2 oz. chocolate, unsweetened
½ cup shortening
1½ cups flour
2 tsps. baking powder
½ tsp. salt
¾ cup sugar
2 eggs

½ cup milk
1 tsp. vanilla
Syrup:
½ cup water
1 rounded tbls. cocoa
1 cup sugar
1 tsp. vanilla
½ tsp. salt

Melt chocolate; mix with melted shortening. Combine flour, baking powder, salt and sugar. Beat eggs; add dry ingredients alternately with milk. Add chocolate mixture and vanilla. Blend well. Bake in waffle iron. Makes 4. Serve warm with syrup. Syrup: In a saucepan, cook water and cocoa for 3 minutes; add sugar, salt, and vanilla. Cook 1 minute more. May be served with ice cream on top.

CHOCOLATE MUD CAKE

1½ sticks margarine, melted
1 cup pecans, chopped
1 cup flour
1 8-oz. pkg. cream cheese
1 cup confectioner's sugar

1 cup whipped topping
1 3-oz. pkg. instant chocolate pudding
1 3-oz. pkg. instant vanilla pudding
4 cups milk

Crust: combine margarine, nuts, and flour; press into bottom of a 9″ x 13″ pan. Bake at 350° for 30 minutes. Cool. Mix the cream cheese, sugar, and whipped topping together. Spread over the crust. Combine the chocolate and vanilla pudding mixes; stir in milk; beat for 2 minutes. Pour over the cheese layer. Chill 24 hours. Serves 12.

LEMON LUSA

¼ lb. butter or margarine
¾ cup chopped pecans
1 cup flour
1 cup confectioner's sugar

2 cups whipped topping
1 8-oz. pkg. cream cheese
2 3-oz. pkgs. instant lemon pudding
3 cups milk

Combine margarine, flour, and ½ cup of the pecans; press into bottom of a 9" x 13" pan. Bake at 350° for 15 to 20 minutes. Cool. Mix the confectioner's sugar, **one** cup of whipped topping, and the cream cheese until well blended. Spread over the cooled crust. Combine the 2 packages of lemon pudding with the 3 cups of milk. Beat for 2 minutes; spread over the cheese layer. Spread the second cup of whipped topping over the pudding layer. Sprinkle with ¼ cup of chopped nuts. Chill. Serves 12.

PISTACHIO WIZZIE

¼ lb. margarine
1 cup flour
¾ cup chopped walnuts
1 cup confectioner's sugar

1 8-oz. pkg. cream cheese
2 8-oz. containers whipped topping
3 3¾-oz. pkgs. instant pistachio
    pudding
4½ cups milk

Combine margarine, flour, and chopped nuts; press into bottom of 9" x 13" pan. Bake at 350° for 15 minutes. Cool. Blend together 1 cup of confectioner's sugar, the cream cheese, and 1 container of whipped topping. Spread on top of baked crust. Mix the 3 packages of instant pudding with the milk; beat until of spreading consistency. Spread over the cheese layer. Cover with the second container of whipped topping. Sprinkle with additional chopped nuts if desired. Refrigerate overnight or for 24 hours. Serves 12.

LEMON TARTS

1 cup sugar
1 lemon — juice and grated rind
1 tbls. flour

2 eggs
1 tbls. butter
pie crust for 8 miniature tart shells

Cream butter and sugar; add lemon juice and rind, flour, and eggs. Blend thoroughly; pour into tart shells. Bake at 350° for 15 to 20 minutes. Check often. Makes 8 miniature tarts.

CHESS TART

Uncooked pie dough
3 tbls. flour
3 cups brown sugar
3 tbls. milk

½ tsp. vanilla
3 eggs
¼ lb. butter
1 tsp. lemon juice

Mix in order given and bake in uncooked pie shell at 450° for 8 to 10 minutes until set, then at 350° about 12 minutes until brown. Check often. Pecans may be put on top if desired. Makes 18 small tarts or 2 large tarts.

BANBURY TARTS (TURNOVERS)

1 pkg. seeded raisins
1 cup sugar
1 lemon — juice and grated rind

1 egg
Uncooked pastry, medium rich

Mix raisins, sugar, lemon juice and rind, and egg; blend well. Roll out pastry; cut into saucer-size rounds. Put 1 tablespoon of raisin mix in center of each round. Fold pastry over mixture, pressing edges together with fork and wetting to seal. Bake on baking sheets for about 20 minutes at 250°; do not allow to brown too much. Makes about 30 turnovers.

CRANBERRY TARTS

2 cups jellied cranberry sauce
1 3-oz. pkg. cream cheese
¼ cup confectioner's sugar
12 marshmallows, diced

½ cup chopped nuts
1 cup heavy cream, whipped
8 baked 3-inch tart shells

Beat cranberry sauce and cream cheese together until well blended. Stir in sugar, marshmallows, and nuts. Fold in the whipped cream. Pile into tart shells. Serves 8.

CHOCOLATE CHESS PIE

¼ lb. butter
1½ squares unsweetened chocolate
1 cup light brown sugar
½ cup granulated sugar
1 tsp. vanilla

1 tbls. flour
2 eggs
½ eggshell of milk
unbaked pastry shell

Melt butter with chocolate. Add brown sugar plus granulated sugar and flour. Beat in the eggs, milk, and 1 teaspoon of vanilla. Pour into pie shell and bake 35 to 40 minutes at 325°. Serves 6.

GRASSHOPPER PIE

2 tbls. melted butter
1¼ cups chocolate wafer crumbs
3 cups mini marshmallows
½ cup milk

1 jigger of crème de cacao
1 jigger of crème de menthe
1 cup of heavy cream, whipped

Mix butter and crumbs and press into 9″ pie pan. Refrigerate 1 hour. Melt marshmallows in milk in top of a double boiler. Cool and add liqueurs. Fold in whipped cream when the milk mixture thickens. Fill pie shell and top with shaved bitter chocolate. Refrigerate at least 1 hour or until ready to serve. Serves 6.

DAIQUIRI PIE

1 envelope plain gelatin	½ cup fresh lime juice
¼ cup cold water	1 tsp. lime rind, grated finely
3 egg yolks	⅓ cup white rum
1 cup sugar	3 egg whites
1 tsp. salt	1 baked pastry shell
green food coloring	½ pt. heavy cream, whipped

Sprinkle gelatin over water; let stand to soften. Put egg yolks, ⅔ cup of sugar, salt, and lime juice in top of a double boiler; beat until well blended. Set over hot water, stirring constantly. Cook until mixture has a custard consistency and coats a spoon. Remove from heat; add softened gelatin, stirring until gelatin is dissolved. Add rind. Add one or two drops of green food coloring to tint the mixture a delicate shade of green. Cool. Stir in rum. Chill mixture until partially set. Whip egg whites until stiff but not dry; gradually beat the remaining ⅓ cup of sugar into whites. Fold in the lime mixture lightly. Pour into the baked pie shell; chill until firm. Before serving, spread with whipped cream, sweetened to taste. Serves 6 to 8.

IMPOSSIBLE APPLE PIE

5 peeled, sliced apples	1 cup flour
1 tbls. sugar	½ cup nuts
1 tsp. cinnamon	1 beaten egg
¾ cup butter (or margarine)	pinch of salt
1 cup sugar	1 9″ pie plate

Fill a 9″ pie plate ⅔ full of sliced apples. Sprinkle tablespoons of sugar and cinnamon over apples. Melt margarine or butter, add sugar, beaten egg, flour, salt, and nuts. Blend well. Pour the batter over apples, spread to cover. Bake at 350° for about 40 minutes. Some of batter will go through to bottom. Serves 6 to 8.

CHOCOLATE VELVET PIE

1½ cups graham cracker crumbs
½ cup melted butter
1 6-oz. pkg. semi-sweet
　chocolate bits
1 8-oz. pkg. cream cheese, softened
½ cup sugar
1 tsp. vanilla or Amoretto

pinch of salt
2 egg yolks
1 cup heavy cream, whipped
2 egg whites
¼ cup sugar

Combine cracker crumbs and butter; press onto bottom and sides of a 10″ pie plate; freeze. Melt chocolate; set aside to cool. Cream together the cream cheese and ½ cup of sugar; add vanilla or Amoretto and the salt. Add the egg yolks one at a time, beating well after each. Stir in the melted chocolate; chill until slightly thickened; whip until smooth. Fold in the whipped cream. Beat the egg whites until foamy; gradually add ¼ cup of sugar; continue beating until the whites are stiff. Fold whites into the chocolate mixture. Pour into pie crust; freeze. Remove from freezer 5 to 10 minutes before serving. Top with additional whipped cream and toasted almond slivers. Serves 8 to 10.

BLUEBERRY GLACÉ PIE

3 cups blueberries
¾ cup water
1 tbls. butter
1 cup sugar

3 tbls. cornstarch
dash of salt
1 tsp. lemon juice
9″ baked pie shell

Put 1 cup blueberries and ¾ cup water in pan and bring to boil. Cook gently about 4 minutes and add 1 tablespoon of butter. Mix 1 cup sugar, 3 tablespoons cornstarch, and dash of salt. Add dry mixture to hot blueberry mixture, stirring constantly. Cook slowly until thick and clear. Remove from heat; add 1 teaspoon lemon juice. Pour over remaining 2 cups blueberries; mix gently. Turn into 9″ baked pie shell. Refrigerate or leave at room temperature. Serve with sweetened whipped cream or vanilla ice cream. Serves 6.

RAISIN PECAN PIE

1 cup pecans
1 cup raisins
1 cup sugar
2 eggs

½ tsp. each of cinnamon, cloves, and
   allspice
1½ tbls. vinegar
1 tbls. melted butter
8″ pie shell, uncooked

Mix all ingredients and pour into 8″ pie shell. Bake at 350° for 30 minutes or until done.

DIXIE PECAN PIE

3 eggs, well beaten
1 cup light or dark corn syrup
½ cup sugar
¼ tsp. salt
¼ cup melted butter or margarine

1 tsp. vanilla or ¼ tsp. almond extract
1 cup pecan meats
pastry for 1-crust pie, 8″

Line an 8-inch pie plate with pastry, fluting the edges. Combine eggs, corn syrup, sugar, salt, and margarine; mix well. Add flavoring and nut meats; pour into pastry shell. Bake at 450° for 10 minutes. Reduce heat to 350° and bake 30 to 35 minutes longer or until knife inserted in center comes out clean. Cool. Serve plain, with whipped cream, or with ice cream. Serves 6.

CHOCOLATE PECAN PIE

1 unbaked 9″ pie crust	3 eggs
2 squares unsweetened chocolate	½ tsp. salt
3 tbls. butter	1 tsp. vanilla
1 cup light corn syrup	1½ cups pecans
¾ cup sugar	

Melt chocolate and butter in small saucepan. Set aside. Combine corn syrup and sugar; boil for 2 minutes, stirring occasionally. Add chocolate to syrup mixture; cool. When filling is at room temperature, beat in eggs one at a time; blend well. Add salt, vanilla, and pecans. Pour into unbaked crust. Bake at 375° for 25 to 30 minutes. Serve warm with vanilla or coffee ice cream. Serves 6 to 8.

PEANUT BUTTER PIE

½ cup creamy peanut butter	8 or 9 oz. prepared whipped topping
½ cup apricot preserves	1 graham cracker crust
½ cup milk	

Blend peanut butter and apricot preserves. Dribble milk over the above and blend. Add topping and blend all together. Place in graham cracker crust and freeze. Serve from freezer.

OLD SALEM THIN VANILLA WAFERS

½ cup butter
⅓ cup sugar
1 egg, well beaten

¾ cup sifted flour
1 tsp. vanilla
pinch of salt (optional)

Mix ingredients in order given. Drop from tip of a spoon onto a cookie sheet. Spread very thin, using a knife dipped in water. Place a pecan half on top of each cookie if desired. Bake at 375° or 400° for 10 to 15 minutes. Watch for oven browning.

BEST-EVER LACE COOKIES

1 cup uncooked quick oatmeal
1 cup sugar
¼ lb. margarine (**not** butter), melted
2 tbls. (heaping) flour
¼ tsp. salt

¼ tsp. baking powder
1 egg, beaten
1 tsp. almond extract
butter

Combine all ingredients; mix well. Place a **buttered** (do **not** use margarine) sheet of foil over a baking sheet. Drop mixture by ¼ teaspoonfuls, 4 inches apart, on foil. Bake 6 to 8 minutes at 350°. Cool on pan for 3 to 4 minutes. Peel or lift off to a cooling rack. Makes 6 to 7 dozen cookies; about 14 per sheet.

SANDTARTS

1 cup butter
½ cup sugar
2 cups flour

¼ tsp. baking powder
½ tsp. rum

Melt butter and let it brown slightly; stir until cold. Add remaining ingredients and mix thoroughly. Chill. Roll out on floured board to ¼-inch thickness. Cut with very small (1-inch diameter) cookie cutter. Bake at 400° for 10 minutes. Makes about 8 dozen.

MARGARET STEWART'S SPICE COOKIES

⅔ cup shortening
1 cup sugar
1 egg
4 tbls. molasses
2 cups flour

1 tsp. soda
1 tsp. cloves
1 tsp. ginger
1 tsp. cinnamon
pinch of salt

Cream shortening with sugar. Add egg and beat well. Add molasses, flour sifted with soda, cloves, ginger, cinnamon, and salt. Mix well. Form into small balls and dip one side in sugar. Place on greased cookie sheet, sugar side up. Flatten and make criss-crosses with a fork. Bake in a 375° oven about 10 minutes. Makes 50 to 75 cookies. Recipe may be doubled. When cookies are cool, place in covered tins to keep crisp.

MRS. JOHANSEN'S ICE-BOX COOKIES

½ lb. butter
1 cup sugar
1 egg
1 tbls. milk

3 cups flour
¾ tsp. vanilla
½ tsp. almond extract

Cream butter; add sugar, egg, milk; add flour and extracts. Divide dough into three sections and roll into cylinders about 1¼" in diameter. Chill until very firm. Cut in ¼" slices and place on greased cookie sheet. Bake at 350° until barely browned.

SPONGE DROPS

3 eggs
1 cup sugar
1 tsp. vanilla

1¼ cups flour
¼ tsp. salt
2 tsps. baking powder

Beat the 3 eggs until very light; gradually add the sugar and vanilla. Sift together the flour, salt, and baking powder; fold into the egg mixture. Let stand 10 minutes. Drop by teaspoonfuls 3 inches apart on lightly greased cookie sheet. Bake at 350° to 375° for about 10 minutes. Remove from pan to rack at once. When cool, sprinkle with powdered sugar.

PEANUT BUTTER COOKIES

1 cup softened peanut butter, smooth or crunchy	1 egg
	1 tsp. vanilla
1 cup sugar	

Beat egg slightly and add all other ingredients. Mix well. Shape into small balls and place on ungreased cookie sheet, leaving a little space between each ball. Flatten slightly with fork, making a crisscross pattern. Bake at 325° for 12 to 15 minutes. Makes about 30 cookies.

BON BON COOKIES

½ cup butter, softened	Icing:
¾ cup confectioner's sugar, sifted	1 cup confectioner's sugar, sifted
1 tbls. vanilla	2 tbls. cream
1½ cups flour, sifted	1 tsp. vanilla
1/8 tsp. salt	food coloring
food coloring, optional OR	1 square unsweetened chocolate
cherries, dates, nuts, pieces of	¼ cup cream
chocolate	Toppings: coconut, nuts, colored sugar

Mix butter, sugar, vanilla, and food coloring. Blend in flour and salt thoroughly. Wrap a level tablespoon of dough around filling (cherry, date, nut, piece of chocolate, etcetera). Bake 1 inch apart on ungreased cookie sheet until set but not brown, about 12 to 15 minutes. Dip tops of warm cookies into icing. Icing: Mix 1 cup sugar, 2 tablespoons cream, vanilla, and food coloring. (For chocolate icing, mix 1 cup sugar, ¼ cup cream, and 1 square of chocolate, melted.) Top each cookie with coconut, nuts, colored sugar, or any other attractive topping. Makes 20 to 25 cookies.

PERSIAN WEDDING CAKES

6 tbls. confectioner's sugar
1 cup butter (not margarine)
1 tsp. vanilla

2 cups cake flour
1 cup chopped pecans
pinch of salt

Cream together the butter, sugar, and vanilla; stir in the flour. Add nuts and mix well. Using 2 teaspoons, shape mixture into 1″ mounds. Bake at 375° for 8 to 10 minutes. Cool and roll in additional confectioner's sugar.

SEABISCUITS

1 cup shortening
1 cup brown sugar
1 cup white sugar
½ tsp. salt
2 eggs

1 tsp. vanilla
1½ cups flour
1 tsp. baking soda
1 tsp. cinnamon
½ cup chopped nuts
4 cups rolled oats

Combine in a mixer the shortening, sugars, salt, eggs, and vanilla. Sift together the flour, baking soda, and cinnamon. Add to mixer ingredients and blend well. Stir in the nuts and rolled oats. Roll into 2-inch balls and flatten with fork on greased cookie sheet. Bake at 350° for 12 to 15 minutes. If desired, raisins or chocolate chips can be added.

CHRISTMAS STOLLEN WREATHS

4½ cups sifted flour	1 cup milk
1 tsp. salt	½ cup sugar
1½ tsps. grated lemon rind	2 pkgs. dry yeast
1 cup butter or margarine	2 eggs, slightly beaten
1 cup chopped mixed candied fruit	melted butter

In a large bowl, combine flour, salt, and lemon rind; cut in the shortening; mix in the candied fruit. Heat milk to lukewarm; add sugar and yeast; stir until dissolved; add eggs. Stir egg mixture into flour mixture. (If dough seems too moist, add up to ½ cup additional flour.) Knead dough on lightly floured board until smooth. Place in a greased bowl; brush with melted butter; cover with a damp cloth. Let rise in warm place until double in bulk or about 2 hours. Turn out on floured board; knead; roll out ½-inch thick. Cut in ½-inch strips 4 to 5 inches long; roll between palms until smooth; form into wreath-like circles on greased baking sheets; moisten ends to seal. Cover and let rise until double in bulk, about ½ hour. Brush with melted butter. Bake at 400° for 15 to 20 minutes or until browned. Frost with ornamental icing; decorate with angelica and cherries. (Half the dough may be used to make one large stollen; bake at 375° for 30 minutes.)

TOFFEE SQUARES

1 cup butter	2 cups flour
1 cup brown sugar, packed	¼ tsp. salt
1 egg yolk	4 ozs. milk chocolate (½ an 8-oz. bar)
1 tsp. vanilla	½ cup chopped nuts

Mix butter, sugar, egg yolk, and vanilla. Stir in flour and salt until well blended. Spread in greased rectangular (13″ x 9″) pan or baking sheet. Bake at 350° for 20 to 25 minutes. Break up pieces of chocolate; place on hot cookies; when soft, spread evenly. Sprinkle with nuts. Cut in bars or squares while warm.

KEVIN'S FAVORITE CHOCOLATE SQUARES

¼ lb. margarine
½ cup salad oil
4 tbls. cocoa
1 cup water
2 cups sugar
2 eggs
½ cup buttermilk or sour milk
2 cups flour

1 tsp. baking soda
1 tsp. vanilla
Frosting:
¼ lb. margarine
4 tbls. cocoa
½ cup buttermilk
1 lb. confectioner's sugar
½ tsp. salt
½ tsp. vanilla

Combine margarine, oil, cocoa, and water in a saucepan over medium heat; stir until completely mixed. Remove from heat; add sugar and milk. Let batter cool slightly; add eggs. Add remaining ingredients and mix thoroughly. Pour into lightly greased and floured 15½" x 10½" jelly roll pan. Bake at 400° for 20 minutes. Frosting: Combine margarine, cocoa, and buttermilk in saucepan; bring to boiling point. Remove from heat; add sugar, salt, and vanilla. Mix thoroughly. Frost cake as soon as it comes out of oven. May be sprinkled with chopped nuts. Cool before cutting.

BROWNIES

2 eggs
1 cup sugar
½ cup flour
2 squares chocolate

½ cup butter
1 tsp. vanilla
1 cup chopped nuts

Beat eggs well; add sugar and flour. Melt together the chocolate and butter and add to egg mixture. Add vanilla and nuts. Bake at 350° for 25 minutes in a 8" x 8" x 2" pan.

ALMOND BARS

½ cup butter
1 cup flour
1 tbls. sugar
2 eggs, beaten
1¼ cups brown sugar
1 cup chopped nuts
1 can coconut

1 tsp. salt
1 tsp. almond extract
Frosting:
1½ cups confectioner's sugar
⅔ cup butter, softened
1 to 2 tbls. evaporated milk or cream
1 tsp. vanilla

Mix butter, flour, and 1 tablespoon of sugar; press into an 8″ square pan; bake at 350° for 10 minutes. Do not cool. Blend the beaten eggs, brown sugar, chopped nuts, coconut, salt, and almond extract; spread over the warm crust. Bake 30 minutes at 350°. Cool. Combine frosting ingredients until creamy. Spread over baked mixture. Cut in bars.

CHERRY-COCONUT BARS

¼ lb. butter
¼ cup confectioner's sugar
1 cup flour
2 eggs, slightly beaten
1 cup sugar
¼ cup flour

½ tsp. baking powder
¼ tsp. salt
1 tsp. vanilla
¾ cup chopped nuts
½ cup coconut
½ cup quartered maraschino cherries

Mix butter, confectioner's sugar, and 1 cup of flour until smooth. Spread over bottom of an 8″ x 8″ pan, pressing smooth with fingers. Bake at 350° for 15 minutes. Stir remaining ingredients into eggs; pour over top of pastry (not necessary to cool). Bake about 25 minutes at 350°. Cool; cut into bars. Makes 18.

MARGARET'S PINKS

½ cup butter
3 tbls. sugar
1 cup flour
jam — strawberry or raspberry
⅓ cup butter
1 cup sugar

2 eggs
1 cup flour
2 tsps. baking powder
¼ tsp. salt
1 tsp. vanilla
½ cup milk
red food coloring

Cream together the first 3 ingredients — butter, sugar, and flour; pat into the bottom of a 9″ x 13″ pan. Spread with a thin layer of jam. Bring the ½ cup of milk to a boiling point; add a couple of drops of red food coloring. Remove from heat and set aside. Cream butter and sugar; add remaining ingredients, including milk; pour over jam layer. Bake at 350° for about 45 minutes. Cut in bars. May be served plain, dusted with confectioner's sugar, or spread with butter icing.

GRAHAM CRACKER SQUARES

4 cups graham cracker crumbs
2 cans condensed milk
1 pkg. chocolate chips

1 tsp. salt
1 cup chopped walnuts
2 tbls. vanilla

Line 9″ square baking pan with waxed paper. Combine and mix well all ingredients; bake at 325° for 30 minutes or until brown on top. Turn upside down on rack; remove paper; turn right side up. Sprinkle with powdered sugar. Cut in squares or bars when cool.

APRICOT BARS

¾ cup dried apricots, diced
¼ cup sugar
1 cup sifted flour
½ cup butter or margarine
⅓ cup sifted flour
½ tsp. baking powder

¼ tsp. salt
2 eggs, beaten
1 cup sugar
½ tsp. vanilla
½ cup chopped nuts
confectioner's sugar

Cover apricots with water; boil 10 minutes; drain. Combine the next three ingredients — ¼ cup sugar, 1 cup sifted flour, and ½ cup butter; press into a 9″-square pan. Bake at 350° for 20 minutes or until lightly brown. Sift ⅓ cup of flour with the baking powder and salt. Beat eggs; add 1 cup of sugar and the sifted flour mixture. Add vanilla, nuts, and cooked apricots. Spread apricot mixture over cooked crust. Bake at 350° for 30 minutes until lightly brown. Cool in pan. Sprinkle with confectioner's sugar. Cut into small squares.

CHOCOLATE KISSES

2 squares chocolate, melted
1 7-oz. pkg. shredded coconut
2 egg whites, stiffly beaten

1 cup confectioner's sugar
1 tbls. flour
½ tsp. vanilla

Add sugar and flour to beaten egg whites; add vanilla. Mix coconut and melted chocolate; add to egg white mixture. Drop by teaspoonfuls on buttered cookie sheet. Bake at 350° for 15 minutes.

QUICKIE MACAROONS

2⅔ cups shredded coconut   1 tsp. vanilla
⅔ cup sweetened condensed milk

Combine coconut, milk, and vanilla; mix well. Drop by teaspoonfuls 1″ apart on greased baking sheets. Bake at 350° for 8 to 10 minutes or until lightly browned. Remove from baking sheets at once. Makes 30.

CHEESECAKE PUFFS

1 lb. cream cheese   1 tsp. vanilla
  (room temperature)   24 vanilla wafers
¾ cup sugar   2 to 3 cans pie filling (cherry,
2 eggs   blueberry, or pineapple)

Whip cream cheese, sugar, eggs, and vanilla together. Place 24 small foil cupcake liners on a cookie sheet or use double paper liners in small cupcake tins. Put a vanilla wafer in each liner. Fill liners ¾ full with cheese mixture. Bake at 375° for 10 minutes. Cool. Put enough pie filling on each to cover or less if preferred. These will keep well in refrigerator for several days. Makes 24.

LACY BOURBON CRISPS

1 6-oz. pkg. semi-sweet
  chocolate bits
1 pkg. all-purpose cookie mix

½ cup bourbon (or rum)
2 tbls. water

Melt chocolate bits over hot, not boiling, water. Combine cookie mix, bourbon, and water; mix well. Blend in the melted chocolate. Drop by **half** teaspoonfuls on an ungreased cookie sheet. Bake in preheated oven at 350° for 5 minutes. Let cool slightly before removing from cookie sheet. (If same sheet is used more than once, wipe dry before re-using.) Makes about 8 dozen.

ORANGE DROP COOKIES

⅔ cup shortening
¾ cup sugar
1 egg
½ cup orange juice
2 tbls. grated orange rind

2 cups flour
½ tsp. baking powder
½ tsp. baking soda
½ tsp. salt

Mix shortening, sugar, and egg. Stir in orange juice and rind. Combine remaining ingredients; add to orange juice mixture. Drop rounded teaspoonfuls 2″ apart on an ungreased cookie sheet. Bake in preheated 400° oven for 8 to 10 minutes. Frost with orange-butter icing. Makes 4 dozen.

ICING

2 cups sifted confectioner's sugar
2 tbls. butter

1 tbls. grated orange rind
2 tbls. orange juice

Combine ingredients; blend until smooth.

RUSSIAN APRICOT COOKIES

6 tbls. butter, softened
½ cup sugar
1 egg yolk
1 tbls. vanilla
1 cup flour
1 tsp. baking powder

½ cup apricot preserves
1 egg white
⅓ cup sugar
1 tsp. cinnamon
⅓ cup chopped nuts

Cream butter and ½ cup sugar; add egg yolk and vanilla; beat well. Sift together the flour and baking powder; add to butter mixture; beat well (it will be flaky); chill overnight. Divide dough in half; roll it on **ungreased** cookie sheet to two 10″ x 6″ x 1/8″ rectangles. Spread apricot preserves on both halves. Beat egg white to soft peaks; add cinnamon and ⅓ cup sugar; beat until stiff. Spread over preserves; sprinkle with nuts. Bake at 350° for 12 minutes. Cool. Cut into bars. Makes 2 dozen.

RUSSIAN SCROLLS

6 cups flour
1 tsp. salt
2 cups shortening
1 cup evaporated milk
6 egg yolks
1 pkg yeast
1 tsp. vanilla

Filling:
1½ lbs. ground nuts
¾ cup brown sugar
¾ cup white sugar
4 tbls. butter
⅔ cup white corn syrup
⅔ cup canned milk or cream

Sift together the flour and salt; add shortening and mix. Beat egg yolks and add ½ cup evaporated milk; dissolve yeast in other half cup of milk. Add both to flour mixture; work until smooth. Cover and refrigerate over night. Roll out on a board until ¼″ thick. Cut into 2- or 3-inch triangles. Filling: Boil sugars, butter, and syrup until soft-ball stage. Cool and add cream. Add nuts. To assemble: put small amount of filling on each triangle and roll up; then roll in granulated sugar and place on cookie sheet. Bake at 400° 10 to 12 minutes.

WALNUT SQUARES

⅓ cup shortening
1½ cups brown sugar firmly packed
½ tsp. salt
1 egg

¾ cup sifted flour
1 tsp. baking powder
1¼ tsp. vanilla extract
¾ cup chopped walnuts

Grease a 7″ x 11″ baking pan. Mix the shortening, 1 cup brown sugar, salt, 1 teaspoon vanilla extract and unbeaten egg yolk together until you have a smooth creamy batter. Sift flour and baking powder together, then beat it into the creamed mixture along with ½ cup chopped walnuts. Spoon dough into the baking pan evenly. Beat the egg white until it stands in points. Then beat in remaining sugar and vanilla until smooth. Spread this topping over the batter. Sprinkle with remaining walnuts. Baqe 35 to 40 minutes in a 325° oven. Cool in pan and cut in 24 squares.

JOE FROGGERS

1 cup shortening
2 cups sugar
¾ cup hot water
¼ cup Rum
2 cups molasses
2 tsps. baking soda

7 cups flour
1 tbls. salt
1 tbls. ginger
1 tsp. clove
1 tsp. nutmeg
½ tsp. allspice

Cream shortening with sugar. Sift dry ingredients. Add alternately to creamed mixture the dry ingredients and the combined liquids. Chill well. Roll ¼″ thick and cut with a 4″ cutter. Bake at 375° for 10 to 12 minutes.

etc.

"STRAWBERRIES"

1 can condensed milk
1 envelope gelatin
2 3-oz. boxes wild strawberry
  gelatin

1 14-oz. pkg. finely shredded
  coconut (not sweetened)
red sugar

Mix all ingredients and refrigerate 4 hours or overnight. Shape into balls, then point to look like strawberries. Roll in red sugar or granulated sugar. Keep refrigerated. Can be frozen. You may add stems and leaves made from gum drops.

QUICK FRENCH CHOCOLATES

8 squares unsweetened chocolate
  (1 pkg.)
6 small Hershey bars

1 14-oz. can condensed milk
chopped pecans or coconut

Melt chocolate and candy bars in top of double boiler. Add the condensed milk and blend well. Shape into balls about the size of a walnut and roll in chopped pecans or coconut. Put on paper towels until cool. Note: it will be easier to make the balls if you grease your hands.

CHOCOLATE WALNUT FUDGE

4½ cups sugar
2 tbls. butter
½ tsp. salt
1 tall can evaporated milk

12 oz. German chocolate (3 bars)
1 12-oz. pkg. semi-sweet chocolate bits
1 pint marshmallow fluff
2 cups chopped walnut meats

Put first 4 ingredients in pan; bring to boil and boil for 8 minutes. In a large bowl put German chocolate, chocolate bits, marshmallow fluff, and nuts. Pour boiling mixture over this and stir until well mixed. Pour into buttered 8″ x 8″ pan. When cool, cut into squares. Makes 4 pounds.

MISS AREY'S CARAMELS

1 cup butter (not margarine)
2 cups sugar
1½ cups white corn syrup
1 cup heavy cream

1 cup milk
4 squares unsweetened chocolate,
   melted
¾ cup chopped pecans
1 tbls. vanilla

Combine the butter, sugar, corn syrup, ½ cup of cream, and ½ cup of milk in heavy saucepan. Bring to a good, rolling boil. Very slowly add the remaining cream and milk. Do **not** allow the boiling to stop. Continue cooking to soft-ball stage when tested in cold water, or until temperature reaches 238° to 240°F. on a candy thermometer. Remove from heat and add chocolate, nuts, and vanilla. Pour into a 9″ x 9″ x 2″ greased pan and chill. When firm, cut in small squares; wrap in waxed paper. Makes 2½ pounds. For vanilla caramels, omit chocolate.

TRUFFLE BUDS

1 8½-oz. pkg. chocolate mint-
flavored wafers
¾ cup coarsely chopped walnuts

1 3-oz. jar candied red cherries,
finely chopped

Melt chocolate wafers in top of a double boiler. Remove from heat; stir in walnuts and cherries. Using 2 teaspoons, fill bite-size, fluted, aluminum-foil cups with mixture. Cool.

FRIENDSHIP CUP

1 cup sugar
½ cup cut-up, well drained
canned peaches

½ cup chunk-style, well drained
pineapple
5 to 7 maraschino cherries cut in half

Combine fruits and sugar in a large glass jar with a cover. Use a wooden spoon. Let stand two weeks, stirring once or twice each week with wooden spoon. Repeat above until your jar is filled. In other words make first batch; before using add at least one more batch. The recipe may be added to at any time the amount in the jar gets low. Use as a sauce for ice cream, angel cake, cottage cheese, or ham.

HOT SHERRIED FRUIT CASSEROLE

1 11-oz. can sliced pineapple, halved	2 tbls. flour
1 11-oz. can peach halves	½ cup brown sugar
1 jar apple rings	¼ lb. butter
1 11-oz. can apricot halves	1 cup medium sherry
1 11-oz. can purple plums, halved and pitted	(not dry)

Arrange fruit in alternating layers in a deep (3″ to 4″) casserole. Other fruits may be substituted, but these give a variety of colors. In a double boiler, combine the flour, sugar, butter, and sherry; cook, stirring, until thickened. Pour over fruit. Cover and refrigerate several hours or overnight. Bake at 350° for 25 to 30 minutes, until bubbly. May be reheated and served again. Serve with chicken or lamb.

STRAWBERRY-RHUBARB JAM

4 cups rhubarb cut in ½″ pieces	1 pkg. strawberry jello
2½ cups granulated sugar	

Bring the rhubarb and sugar slowly to a boil and boil 7 minutes. Add contents of 1 package of strawberry jello and mix well. Pour into jars and keep in refrigerator. May be frozen. Yield — 3½ cups.

SWEET PEPPER JELLY

¾ cup red hot peppers, chopped   1½ cups white vinegar
  (about 20 finger-size)   6½ cups sugar
¾ cup green bell peppers, chopped   1 6-oz. bottle certo
  (about 4 to 6 medium size)   red or green food coloring

Put vinegar and chopped peppers in blender and process until fine. Empty
blender into saucepan and bring contents to a rolling boil. Stir in sugar.
Remove pan from heat when sugar is dissolved. Strain. Cool for 5 minutes at
room temperature; add certo and food coloring; stir to mix thoroughly. Bring
to a boil again, let cool. Fill sterilized jars. Keeps indefinitely.

BASIL JELLY

6½ cups sugar   1 box certo (2 packs)
1 cup cider vinegar   green food coloring
2 cups water   1 cup tightly packed fresh basil leaves

Bring to a boil the water, vinegar, sugar, and basil leaves. Hard boil. Add
entire box of certo and boil for one timed minute. Strain and skim; add a
few drops of green food coloring. Pour into 8 jelly glasses that have been
boiled. Add parafin or lids.

CHERYL'S APPLE CHUTNEY

8 cups peeled and cored apples
2 cups seeded light raisins
Peel of 2 oranges, finely chopped
2 cups sugar

½ cup vinegar
⅓ tsp. ground cloves
½ to ¾ cups water

Chop apples; combine in large saucepan with all other ingredients. (Amount of water depends on juiciness of apples.) Bring to a rolling boil; reduce heat to a simmer. Cook until apples are tender. Ladle into hot jars; adjust lids at once. Process in boiling water bath for 5 minutes. Makes 5 to 7 pints.

CHUTNEY

5 lbs. mature green mangoes
2 large onions
2 green peppers
1 cup seeded raisins
½ cup pitted dates
1 tbls. cinnamon
1 tsp. ground cloves
1 tsp. allspice
6 tamarind nuts (may be omitted)

2 tsps. salt
1 cup preserved or crystalized ginger
1 cup near-ripe, chopped papaya
2 cloves chopped garlic
1 lime, seeded and chopped
3 cups brown sugar
1 qt. wine vinegar
¼ tsp. cayenne pepper

Pare and cut mangoes in small slices. Chop onions, peppers, dates, papaya, garlic, and lime; mix with all other ingredients. Bring to a boil. Add more brown sugar to taste. Boil gently for one hour stirring often. Spoon into Mason jals and seal. Makes 2 quarts.

GREEN TOMATO MARMALADE

5 lbs. green tomatoes	2 oranges, juice and rind
4 lbs. sugar	1 pkg. raisins
2 lemons, juice and rind	¼ lb. broken walnut meats

Grate rind of oranges and lemons. Chop tomatoes. Combine fruit juices, rind, tomatoes, and sugar in large kettle; bring to a slow boil. Cook, stirring frequently, for 1½ hours, uncovered. Add raisins and walnut meats. Cook for 20 minutes longer. Pour into sterilized glasses; cover with paraffin at once. Makes about 8 glasses.

SANDWICH LOAF

1 loaf sandwich bread, unsliced	1 cup chopped pecans
1 can shrimp	1 small can crushed pineapple, drained
3 hard-boiled eggs	2 cups finely chopped chicken
¼ cup chopped celery	6 slices crisp bacon, crumbled
mayonnaise	½ jar pimientoes, chopped
lemon juice	3 tbls. chopped almonds
1 8-oz. pkg. cream cheese	2 8-oz. pkgs. cream cheese

Remove all crust from bread; slice lengthwise into 4 layers. First layer: chop shrimp and eggs; add celery; bind with mayonnaise to which a few drops of lemon juice have been added. Second layer: 1 package cream cheese, softened; add pecans and pineapple. Third layer: Mix chicken, bacon, pimiento, and almonds; bind with mayonnaise. Top with fourth slice of bread. Frost with 2 packages of cream cheese, to which enough cream is added to make it spreadable. Green or yellow food coloring may be added to cheese. Serves 10 to 12.

CHOCOLATE SAUCE

4 squares unsweetened chocolate
1 cup sugar
1 5⅓-oz. can evaporated milk

1 tbls. black coffee
1 tsp. vanilla

Melt chocolate in top of a double boiler; add sugar and mix well. Cook covered for ½ hour. Add milk, coffee, and vanilla. Beat well. Cool and refrigerate. To serve, reheat in double boiler.

RICH CHOCOLATE SAUCE

2 ozs. chocolate, unsweetened
¼ cup butter
1½ cups sugar

½ can evaporated milk
½ tsp. vanilla

Melt the butter over low heat; add the chocolxte. When both are melted, stir in sugar gradually and continue to stir until the sugar is dissolved. Stir in evaporated milk. Remove from the stove and stir in vanilla. Makes about 1 pint. Can be stored in refrigerator; reheat for serving.

BUTTERSCOTCH SAUCE

¾ cup light brown sugar
½ cup corn syrup
¼ cup water

3 tbls. butter
½ cup evaporated milk
½ tsp. vanilla

Put the sugar, corn syrup, water, and butter in a saucepan; stir over low heat until the sugar is dissolved. Boil until the mixture forms a very soft ball in cold water. Remove from the stove; stir in the milk and vanilla.

KENTUCKY SAUCE

1 cup brown sugar
1 cup white sugar
1 cup water
1 cup pecans, broken

1 cup strawberry preserves
1 orange
1 lemon
1 cup Bourbon

Combine the brown sugar, white sugar, and water; cook until syrup reaches about 240° on candy thermometer or until it will almost spin a thread. Remove from heat and stir in the pecans and strawberry preserves. Remove rind from orange and lemon with a potato peeler and chop fine. Cut off and discard white membrane; remove fruit sections. Cut or chop sections into small pieces. Add to syrup mixture along with the Bourbon. Refrigerate. Makes 1 quart. Serve over ice cream. Keeps indefinitely.

BLUEBERRY SAUCE

½ cup butter
1 cup sugar
3 tbls. flour

1 cup boiling water
1 cup crushed blueberries
with juice

Cream the butter and sugar; work in the flour; add the boiling water and then the blueberries with juice. Cook and stir until thick.

TOMATO JUICE

1 peck (12 lbs.) ripe tomatoes
4 medium onions, sliced
12 sprigs parsley
2 bay leaves
1 tbls. sugar

1 tsp. pepper corns
1 tsp. celery seeds
1 tsp. cloves (heads removed)
2 tbls. salt

Cut up tomatoes; cut out hard white parts. Place all ingredients in large kettle. Simmer for ½ hour. Turn up heat and let come to a rolling boil. Remove from heat; strain. Fill sterilized jars to top. Seal. Makes 6 pints.

Notes

CONTRIBUTORS

Marjorie Allard
Mrs. M. Alsberg
Mrs. W.B. Bacon
Rose Baldwin
Mrs. J. Ballou
Mrs. A.P. Barton
Bertha Bixby
Mrs. O.K. Black
Mrs. J.W. Bolton
Grace Boremi
Joan Boudreau
Mrs. H.J. Bourneuf, Jr.
Mrs. F. Brown, Jr.
Mrs. E.T. Breed
Mrs. R.P. Breed*
Mrs. R.P. Breed, III
Mrs. R.P. Breed, Jr.
Mimi T. Breed
Mrs. W.J. Breed
Mrs. J. Burbidge*
Mrs. W. Callahan*
Mrs. W.T. Carpenter
Judy Carpenter
Mrs. Mario Ciullo
Mrs. H.W. Cogger
Mrs. S.A. Comins
Mrs. P. Conley*
Mrs. W.H. Cook
Mrs. L.C. Copeland
Mrs. J.E. Coppola
Mrs. F.P. Costanza
Mrs. W. Cox*
Mrs. W. Creamer
Mrs. N.J. Darling, Jr.
Virginia P. Davenport
Nelson L. Dionne
Mrs. A. Donovan*
Mrs. T.F. Downey
Mrs. R.A. Duffill
Joyce E. Duffy
Barbara L. Eaton
Caroline Fabyan
Kathie Fallon
Carolyn Farley
Mrs. D. Francescon
Mrs. W.K. Freeman

Mrs. T. Frothingham, 3rd
Mrs. S.N. Gardner
Mrs. Paul Giles
Mrs. Catherine B. Gill
Mrs. W.T. Gill, II
Constance Godfrey
Beatrice M. Goldsmith
Albert Goodue
Mrs. Albert Goodue
Carol L. Guanci
Mrs. J. Haug
Mary Hanlon
Mrs. H. Hazen, Jr.*
Mrs. R.S. Herbst
Ronni Hoover
Mrs. H. Houlberg
Raymona Hull
Marcia J. Hunkins
Edna Jewett
Mrs. W.E. Johnson
Dorothy Johnson
Mrs. T. Johnson
Mrs. C.K. Jones
Mrs. J.L. Kearney
Dora Keay
Donald S. Kenney
Mrs. L.B. Kilgore
Arakel Krikorian
Shelia Krikorian
Mrs. D.A. Lail
Mrs. G.G. Lail*
Mrs. P.H. Lord
William C. Loring
Sally Loring
Mrs. E. Low
William MacLean
Virginia L. MacKeen
M.E. Mahoney
Edna L. Maitland
Mrs. S.G. Markin
Mrs. E.F. Marquis
Mrs. James A. Marsh
Mrs. W.M. Marsh
Mrs. J.J. Matula
Marion McDonald
Mrs. W.M. McKim

CONTRIBUTORS

Mrs. R.K. Moore
Mrs. J.A. Morrison*
Mrs. J.A. Morrison, Jr.
Mrs. H.A. Morss, Jr.
Mrs. W.T. Moulton*
Mrs. W.T. Moulton, Jr.*
Bettine Norton
Pauline M. Nickerson
Bradford C. Northrup
Lydia P. Ogilby
Mrs. R.L. Osgood
Mrs. R.W. Osgood, 3rd*
Cornelia D. Ostheimer
Mrs. E.T. Oliver
Mrs. A. Patton
Judy Perkins
Mrs. G.A. Peterson*
Mrs. D.K. Phillips
Mrs. E.L. Pierson
Molly Pitcher
Mrs. D. Pitman
Mrs. L. Pocharski*
Mrs. J.H. Pramberg
Mrs. M.A. Princi
Adele Pulitzer
Jane Reed
Kit Richardson
B.A. Riemer
Mrs. J.C. Roper, Jr.*
Mary A. Roper
Susan M. Roper
Donna Rotcavich
Virginia N. Salomon
W.L. Saltonstall
Mrs. P.B. Sargent
Lee Sausele
Mrs. J.E. Sayer

Mrs. W.A. Slade, Jr.
Mrs. D.B. Smith*
Mrs. H.O. Smith
Jody Smith
Mary S. Smith*
Mrs. G. Smith
Barbara Speer
Vera Stanhope
Mrs. W.A. Stanley
Sandy Stark
Lynn St. Clair
Mrs. R.A. St. Germain
Margaret W. Strath
Rilda Stuart*
Helen Thompson
Mrs. C. Thompson
Mrs. B.F. Tolles, Jr.
Thayer Tolles
Mrs. James Totten
Mrs. G.B. Townsend
Gay Tracy
Mrs. E Tufts
Thelma S. Turner
Mrs. P.N. Walker
Anne Watson
Lea D. Watson*
Mrs. M. Weaver
Deborah Wender
Mrs. P.B. Weld
Mrs. R.S. West*
Barbara White
Mrs. J.A. Wiese*
Mrs. J.R. Wilson*
Mrs. T. Wingardner
Mrs. N. Xanthaky*
Mrs. D.K. Young

The Ladies Committee was delighted by the quantity and quality of the recipes submitted for *Served in Salem;* difficult choices were made to eliminate duplication and to achieve diversification. We thank you one and all.

An asterisk has been placed by the names of those ladies who tested recipes.